PLASTIC CANVAS

Santa SURPRISES

the Needlecraft Shop

Publisher: DONNA ROBERTSON

Design Director: FRAN ROHUS

Production & Photography Director:
ANGE VAN ARMAN

EDITORIAL

Senior Editor: JANET TIPTON

Editor: KRIS KIRST

Assistant Graphics Editors:
JEANNE AUSTIN, GLENDA CHAMBERLAIN,
SANDI HITT, DEBBY KEEL

Copy Editor: DIANA KORDSMEIER

PRODUCTION

Book Design & Production:
GLENDA CHAMBERLAIN

Production Team:
BETTY RADLA, CATHY DRENNAN

PHOTOGRAPHY

Photography Coordinator/Stylist:
RUTH WHITAKER

Assistant Photo Stylist: JAN JAYNES

Photographers:
RUSSELL CHAFFIN, KEITH GODFREY

Cover Photograph:
RUSSELL CHAFFIN

PRODUCT DESIGN

Design Coordinator: PAM PRATHER

BUSINESS

C.E.O: JOHN ROBINSON

Vice President/Marketing: GREG DEILY

CREDITS

Sincerest thanks to all the designers, manufacturers
and other professionals whose dedication
has made this book possible. Special thanks to
David Norris and Kaye Stafford of Quebecor
Printing Book Group, Kingsport, TN.

Library of Congress
Cataloging-in-Publication Data

ISBN: 1-57367-095-2
First Printing: 1997
Library of Congress Catalog
Card Number: 97-68263
Published and Distributed by
The Needlecraft Shop, LLC, Big Sandy, Texas 75755
Printed in the United States of America.

Dear Friend,

What is the magic that surrounds the Christmas holiday? Could it be the expectation that is built around the celebration? Is it the amount of time and energy that we invest in the preparation? I think the planning, shopping and decorating that lead up to that special day all contribute to the wonder.

It seems as if the Christmas season is the time when the child in each of us is reborn. It's a time when the sights, sounds and tastes of the season titillate our senses with excitement and anticipation as we look forward to Christmas morning. No matter how much we hear the Scrooges around us moan and groan about the effort they must put forth to make the day come together, those of us who love the celebration process never lose our love for this joyful time that brings the splendor of childhood dreams to life.

And, long after we've discovered the fable behind the existence of Santa, we never turn down a single gift he wishes to give us. Nor do we ever tire of seeing our loved ones' eyes light up with delight when they discover the surprises that we, as Santa's helpers, bring to them.

You hold in your hands a treasury of needlecraft designs that will make your Holiday planning easier than ever. Page after colorful page is packed with delightful products and ideas that will not only thrill you, but can add charm and vibrance to your celebration, too. *Santa Surprises* is one of those collections of gifts and decorative ideas that a Santa's helper can't be without. Enjoy the dreaming as you turn the pages. Make your plans to join the ranks of Santa's helpers and bring all of *Santa Surprises* to life.

Merry Stitching to All,

Donna

Donna Robertson

Contents

Charming St. Nick

Christmas Spirits 8
Country Santa 12
Santa's Watching 14
Nesting Santas. 20
Santa's Place Mat. 22
Winter Wizard 24
Tyrolean Match Holder 26

Frosty Friends

Percival Penguin 32
Wintery Wreath. 34
I Love Snow 38
Mini Frosty Basket 39
Penguin Party 40
Christmas Wall Hanging . . . 45
Warm Winter Friends 46

Yuletide Traditions

Bells & Bows. 52
Poinsettias 'round the Room 54
Season's Greetings Cap 56
Ornament Coasters 62
Gift Wrapped Doorstop 63
Country Christmas Kitchen 64
Country Decor 68

Gifts from Santa

Merry Lights Earrings 72
"Ho Ho Ho" Pin 73
Candy Cane Earrings 73
Precious Pet 74
Bougainvillea Frame 78

Nutcracker Soldier 80
Chef Piggy 82
Rustic Lodge Canisters 89

Christmas Spirit

Celestial Messengers 96
Angelic Doorstop 98
Musical Spirits 100
Stained Glass Tote 103
Bejeweled Angel 106
Christmas Advent Calendar . 108

Santa Treats

Doorknob
Basket 114
Christmas Tic-Tac-Toe 116
Bathtime Fun 117
Clown Collector 120
Christmas Candy Boxes 122
Southern Belle 124

Festive Trimmings

Pretty Pinecones 132
Elegant Snow Angels 134
Lil' Package Ornaments 136
Yuletide Warmers 137
Snowy Evergreen 138
Festive Touches 140
Christmas Candles 141
Shimmering Shapes 144
Tropical Holiday Decor 147
Pearls & Lace 148

General Instructions 154
Stitch Guide 157
Acknowledgments 158
Index 160

Christmas Spirits

SIZE: Large Santa is 2¼" x 4" x 7⅞" tall; Medium Santa is 2¾" x 3½" x 6¾" tall; Small Santa is 1¾" x 3" x 5½" tall.

SKILL LEVEL: Challenging

MATERIALS: Two sheets of 7-count plastic canvas; ¼ sheet of 10-count plastic canvas; Six black 4-mm cabochons; 28 aurora borealis 3-mm round faceted acrylic stones; 25 red 4-mm round faceted acrylic stones; One ¼" x ½" red acrylic star (for top of staff); 18-20 assorted charms and beads (jingle bells, hearts, stars, stones and teddy bear); 2 yds. each gold and pearl fine metallic braid; Polyester fiberfill; Craft glue or glue gun; GlissenGloss™ Estaz (for amount see Color Key on page 10); Medium metallic braid (for amount see Color Key); #3 pearl cotton (for amounts see Color Key); Worsted-weight or plastic canvas yarn (for amounts see Color Key).

CUTTING INSTRUCTIONS:

NOTES: Graphs on pages 10 & 11.

Use 10-count canvas for F and G pieces.

A: For Large, Medium and Small Santa fronts and backs, cut two each (one for each front and one for each back) according to graphs.

B: For Large, Medium and Small Santa bases, cut one each according to graphs.

C: For Large, Medium and Small Santa arms, cut two each according to graphs.

D: For Large, Medium and Small Santa shoes, cut two each according to graphs.

E: For Large Santa tree, Medium Santa bag and Small Santa package, cut two each according to graphs.

F: For faces, cut three according to graph.

G: For Large, Medium and Small Santa mustaches, cut one each according to graphs.

H: For Small Santa staff, cut two 2 x 29 holes (no graph).

STITCHING INSTRUCTIONS:

1: Using colors (substitute main coat color for white center Continental Stitches on each back) and stitches indicated, work A pieces according to graphs. Using colors and stitches indicated, work B-G (one of each C on opposite side of canvas) pieces according to graphs; with white pearl cotton for faces and with matching colors, Overcast unfinished edges of C, D, F and G pieces. Using dk. brown and Continental Stitch, work H pieces.

2: Using colors and embroidery stitches indicated, embroider detail on A (continue embroidery across center back), C and F pieces as indicated on graphs. (**NOTE:** For each nose, use four Straight Stitches.)

3: With matching colors, Whipstitch corresponding A and B pieces wrong sides together as indicated, stuffing with fiberfill before closing. With dk. royal, Whipstitch bag E pieces wrong sides together as indicated, stuffing with fiberfill; Overcast unfinished edges. With matching colors for tree and red for package, Whipstitch corresponding E pieces wrong sides together. With dk. brown, Whipstitch H pieces wrong sides together.

4: Glue two black beads to each face for eyes as shown in photo. For Small Santa, glue one 3-mm stone at intersection of each embroidered star on front, back and arms. Glue 4-mm stones to one side of tree as indicated.

NOTE: Cut gold and pearl fine metallic braid into 12" lengths.

Continued on page 10

Wrapping Creatively

LACE HANKY – Add an unexpected gift to a package by attaching a lace-edged handkerchief and tiny dried flowers to a wrapped package.

Christmas Spirits

Continued from page 8

5: Holding four of each color braid strand together, wrap around tapered end of bag and tie into a knot; tie 8 to 10 charms to cord ends as desired. Thread remaining cord strands through each hole at one end of staff; tie a charm to each end. Glue a charm to top of bag, and glue ¼" x ½" red acrylic star to top of staff as shown.

6: Glue one mustache to each face and corresponding C-F pieces to Santa bodies as shown; glue staff to one arm and one shoe of Small Santa as shown. Tie remaining pearl medium metallic braid into a bow and trim ends; glue to top of package as shown.✻

– Designed by Vicki Blizzard

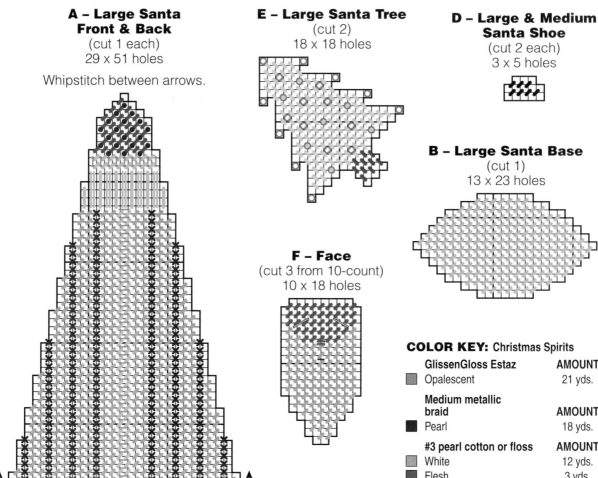

A – Large Santa Front & Back
(cut 1 each)
29 x 51 holes

Whipstitch between arrows.

Whipstitch to B.

E – Large Santa Tree
(cut 2)
18 x 18 holes

D – Large & Medium Santa Shoe
(cut 2 each)
3 x 5 holes

B – Large Santa Base
(cut 1)
13 x 23 holes

F – Face
(cut 3 from 10-count)
10 x 18 holes

COLOR KEY: Christmas Spirits

GlissenGloss Estaz			AMOUNT
Opalescent			21 yds.
Medium metallic braid			**AMOUNT**
Pearl			18 yds.
#3 pearl cotton or floss			**AMOUNT**
White			12 yds.
Flesh			3 yds.
Dk. Red			1 yd.

Worsted-weight	Nylon Plus™	Need-loft®	YARN AMOUNT
Dk. Green	#31	#27	33 yds.
Dk. Royal	#07	#48	31 yds.
Dk. Red	#20	#01	28 yds.
White	#01	#41	27 yds.
Dk. Brown	#36	#15	4 yds.
Black	#02	#00	3 yds.

STITCH KEY:
- — Backstitch/Straight Stitch
- ● French Knot
- ○ Red Stone Placement

C – Large Santa Arm
(cut 2)
9 x 14 holes

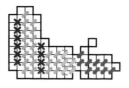

G – Large Santa Mustache
(cut 1 from 10-count)
7 x 15 holes

A – Medium Santa Front & Back
(cut 1 each)
25 x 43 holes

Whipstitch between arrows.

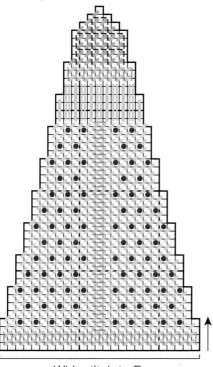

Whipstitch to B.

G – Medium Santa Mustache
(cut 1 from 10-count)
7 x 9 holes

C – Medium Santa Arm
(cut 2)
8 x 13 holes

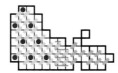

E – Medium Santa Bag
(cut 2)
19 x 22 holes

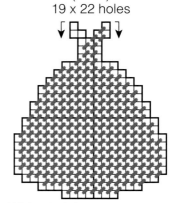

Whipstitch between arrows.

B – Medium Santa Base
(cut 1)
11 x 19 holes

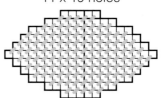

B – Small Santa Base
(cut 1)
9 x 17 holes

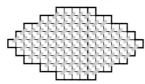

C – Small Santa Arm
(cut 2)
7 x 11 holes

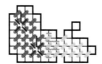

D – Small Santa Shoe
(cut 2)
2 x 5 holes

G – Small Santa Mustache
(cut 1 from 10-count)
7 x 9 holes

E – Small Santa Package
(cut 2)
6 x 9 holes

A – Small Santa Front & Back
(cut 1 each)
21 x 35 holes

Whipstitch between arrows.

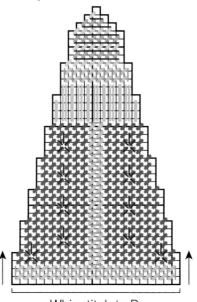

Whipstitch to B.

Country Santa

SIZE: $1\frac{1}{2}$" x $10\frac{3}{4}$" x 13".

SKILL LEVEL: Challenging

MATERIALS: Two 12" x 18" or larger sheets of stiff 7-count plastic canvas; One sheet of regular flexibility 7-count plastic canvas; Seven 9-mm jingle bells; Victorian white Rainbow™ hair by Kunin Felt; 4" length of brown-stained $\frac{3}{16}$" wooden dowel; Craft glue or glue gun; $\frac{1}{16}$" ribbon floss (for amounts see Color Key on page 17); Bumples™ bumpy doll hair by One & Only Creations® or textured yarn (for amount see Color Key); Worsted-weight or plastic canvas yarn (for amounts see Color Key).

CUTTING INSTRUCTIONS:

NOTES: Graphs & diagrams on pages 17-19.

Use stiff for A-F and regular flexibility canvas for remaining pieces.

A: For cow side #1, cut two according to graph.

B: For cow side #2, cut two according to graph.

C: For cow left rear inner leg, cut one according to graph.

D: For cow right rear inner leg, cut one according to graph.

E: For cow left front inner leg, cut one according to graph.

F: For cow right front inner leg, cut one according to graph.

G: For cow chest piece, cut one according to graph.

H: For cow rear piece, cut one according to graph.

I: For Santa legs, cut two according to graph.

J: For Santa arms, cut two according to graph.

K: For hen wings, cut two according to graph.

L: For cow ears, cut two according to graph.

M: For tree, cut two according to graph.

N: For cow collar, cut one 3 x 45 holes (no graph).

STITCHING INSTRUCTIONS:

1: Using colors and stitches indicated, holding matching pieces together and working as one, work A and B pieces through both thicknesses according to graphs; omitting hair areas, fill in uncoded areas using dk. red and Continental Stitch.

2: Using colors and stitches indicated, work C-M (work one each I-L on opposite side of canvas) pieces according to graphs. With matching colors, Overcast unfinished edges of I-L pieces and indicated edges of C-F pieces. Using red and Continental Stitch, work N piece; Whipstitch ends together and Overcast edges.

NOTE: Cut Bumples™ bumpy doll hair or textured yarn into 6" lengths.

3: Using 6" strands and Lark's Head Knot, work hair areas on A and B pieces according to graphs; trim ends to $1\frac{1}{4}$". Using colors and embroidery stitches indicated, embroider detail on A, B and L pieces as indicated.

NOTE: Cut remaining black yarn into four 18" lengths and remaining white yarn into seven 6" lengths.

4: For tail, holding 18" black strands together, fold in half; insert six 6" white strands through loop and tie together with remaining 6" strand $\frac{1}{2}$" from top, forming tassel. Braid with two groups of three and one group of two black strands to a 3" length; tie ends into a knot.

5: Whipstitch and assemble A-H pieces and tail according to Country Santa Assembly Diagram on page 19.

6: With green, Whipstitch M pieces wrong sides together as indicated; Overcast unfinished edges.

Tiny Tree Trimmings

LET IT SNOW – Decorate a tiny tree with drifts of artificial snowflakes and ice skate or snow ski charms as ornaments. Wrap a scarf around the base for a cozy winter look.

Travel with old farmer Santa to Christmas lands rich with milk and honey.

NOTE: Pull out and form four long tufts of Rainbow™ hair.

7: Glue one tuft of hair around each arm and leg for cuffs as shown in photo. Glue dowel to inside of tree leaving a 1¾" trunk. Glue arms and legs to Santa body and tree trunk between hands as shown.

8: For collar, starting at third hole from seam, with red ribbon floss, tack each jingle bell to collar six or seven holes apart. Slip collar over cow head as shown.✹

– *Designed by Darla J. Fanton*

Santa's Watching

SIZE: 8½" x about 17¾".

SKILL LEVEL: Average

MATERIALS: One sheet of 12" x 18" or larger 7-count plastic canvas; One standard-size sheet of 7-count plastic canvas; One 6" piece of floral wire; Craft glue or glue gun; Worsted-weight or plastic canvas yarn (for amounts see Color Key).

CUTTING INSTRUCTIONS:

NOTES: Graphs continued on page 16.
Use large sheet for A.

A: For face, cut one according to graph.

B: For mustache, cut one according to graph.

C: For eyebrows #1 and #2, cut one each according to graphs.

D: For hat trim, cut one according to graph.

E: For hat pom-pom, cut one according to graph.

STITCHING INSTRUCTIONS:

1: Using colors indicated and Continental Stitch, work A-C pieces according to graphs; fill in uncoded areas of A and B pieces using white and Continental Stitch. Using white and Rya Knot (leave ¾" loops), work D and E pieces. Clip through loops and fray ends to fluff. With silver for eyebrows and mustache and with matching colors, Overcast unfinished edges of A-E pieces.

NOTE: Separate remaining black and red into 2-ply or nylon plastic canvas yarn into 1-ply strands.

2: Using 2-ply (or 1-ply) in colors indicated and Backstitch, embroider eye detail on A as indicated on graph.

NOTE: Cut two 3" pieces of floral wire; wrap each around a pencil to form two ½" coils.

3: Glue one coil to center of wrong side of mustache and remaining coil to center of wrong side of pom-pom. Glue mustache coil, eyebrows, hat trim and pom-pom coil to face as shown in photo. (**NOTE:** Coils should allow mustache and pom-pom to move freely.)❋

– Designed by Jacquelyn Fox

D – Hat Trim
(cut 1) 22 x 57 holes

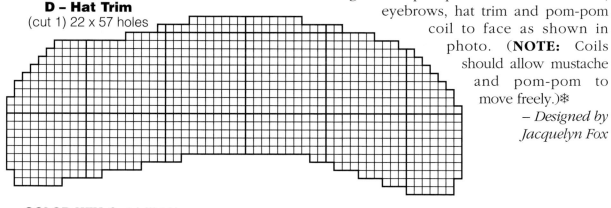

COLOR KEY: Santa's Watching

	Worsted-weight	Nylon Plus™	Need-loft®	YARN AMOUNT
◩	White	#01	#41	2½ oz.
■	Silver	#40	#37	17 yds.
■	Red	#19	#02	16 yds.
▨	Flesh	#14	#56	10 yds.
▨	Dk. Red	#20	#01	5 yds.
■	Coral	–	#65	3 yds.
■	Black	#02	#00	2 yds.
▨	Pink	#11	#07	2 yds.
■	Dusty Blue	#38	#34	1 yd.

STITCH KEY:

— Backstitch/Straight Stitch

B – Mustache (cut 1) 19 x 46 holes

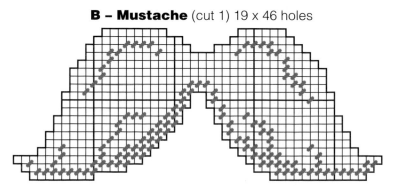

Announce the presence of old St. Nick with a festive door or wall hanging.

Santa's Watching

Instructions & photo on pages 14 & 15

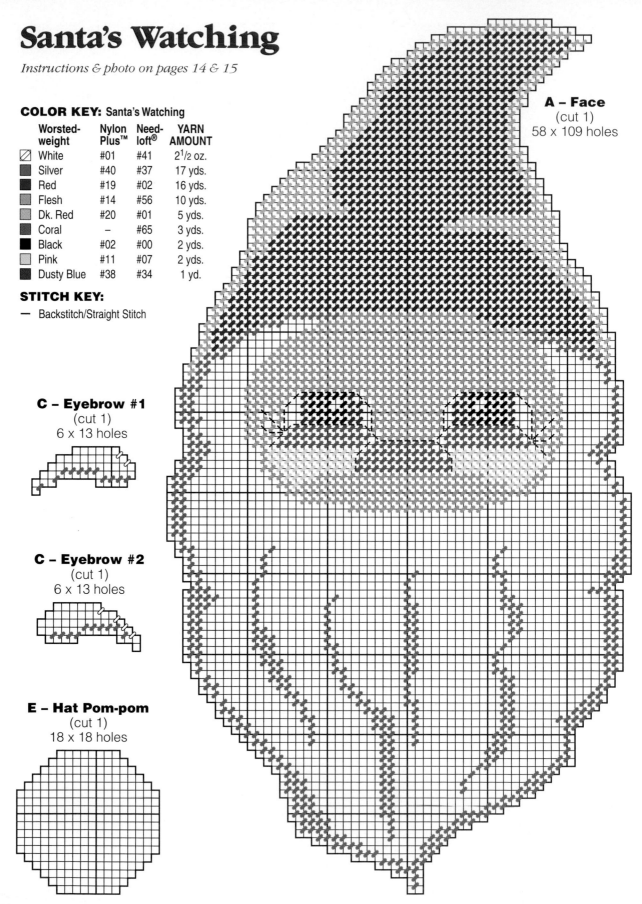

COLOR KEY: Santa's Watching

	Worsted-weight	Nylon Plus™	Need-loft®	YARN AMOUNT
▨	White	#01	#41	2½ oz.
◼	Silver	#40	#37	17 yds.
◼	Red	#19	#02	16 yds.
◼	Flesh	#14	#56	10 yds.
◼	Dk. Red	#20	#01	5 yds.
◼	Coral	–	#65	3 yds.
◼	Black	#02	#00	2 yds.
◻	Pink	#11	#07	2 yds.
◼	Dusty Blue	#38	#34	1 yd.

STITCH KEY:

— Backstitch/Straight Stitch

A – Face
(cut 1)
58 x 109 holes

C – Eyebrow #1
(cut 1)
6 x 13 holes

C – Eyebrow #2
(cut 1)
6 x 13 holes

E – Hat Pom-pom
(cut 1)
18 x 18 holes

Country Santa *Instructions & photo on pages 12 & 13*

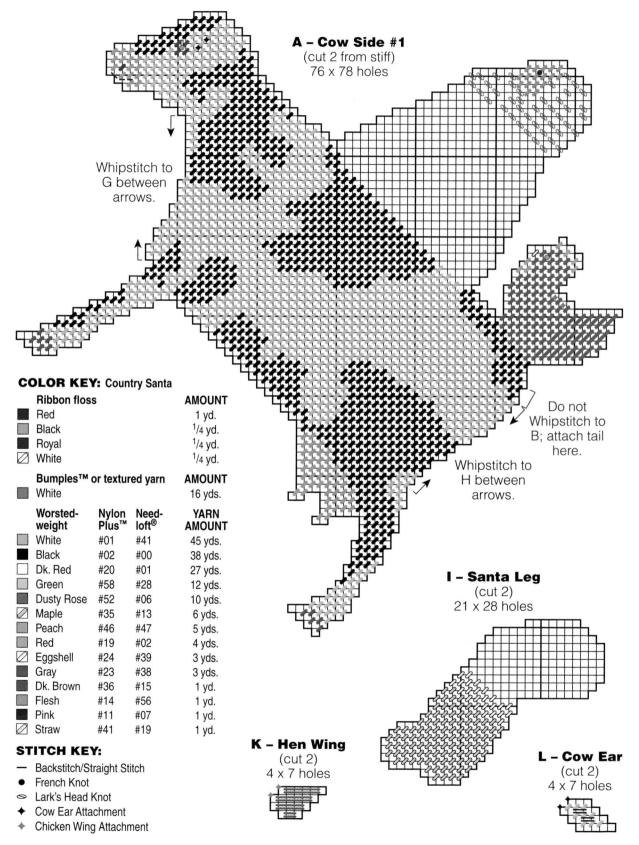

A – Cow Side #1
(cut 2 from stiff)
76 x 78 holes

Whipstitch to G between arrows.

Do not Whipstitch to B; attach tail here.

Whipstitch to H between arrows.

COLOR KEY: Country Santa

Ribbon floss			AMOUNT
■ Red			1 yd.
▨ Black			1/4 yd.
■ Royal			1/4 yd.
▨ White			1/4 yd.

Bumples™ or textured yarn			AMOUNT
▨ White			16 yds.

Worsted-weight	Nylon Plus™	Need-loft®	YARN AMOUNT
▨ White	#01	#41	45 yds.
■ Black	#02	#00	38 yds.
□ Dk. Red	#20	#01	27 yds.
▨ Green	#58	#28	12 yds.
▨ Dusty Rose	#52	#06	10 yds.
▨ Maple	#35	#13	6 yds.
▨ Peach	#46	#47	5 yds.
▨ Red	#19	#02	4 yds.
▨ Eggshell	#24	#39	3 yds.
▨ Gray	#23	#38	3 yds.
▨ Dk. Brown	#36	#15	1 yd.
▨ Flesh	#14	#56	1 yd.
■ Pink	#11	#07	1 yd.
▨ Straw	#41	#19	1 yd.

STITCH KEY:
- — Backstitch/Straight Stitch
- ● French Knot
- ∽ Lark's Head Knot
- ✦ Cow Ear Attachment
- ✦ Chicken Wing Attachment

I – Santa Leg
(cut 2)
21 x 28 holes

K – Hen Wing
(cut 2)
4 x 7 holes

L – Cow Ear
(cut 2)
4 x 7 holes

Country Santa

Instructions & photo on pages 12 & 13

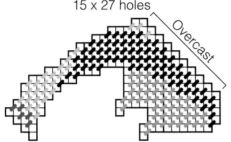

C – Left Rear Inner Leg
(cut 1 from stiff)
15 x 27 holes

Overcast

**D – Right Rear
Inner Leg**
(cut 1 from stiff)
10 x 18 holes

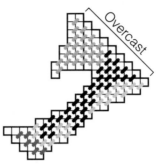

Overcast

E – Left Front Inner Leg
(cut 1 from stiff)
10 x 18 holes

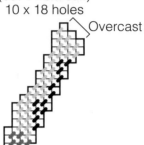

Overcast

B – Cow Side #2
(cut 2 from stiff)
69 x 71 holes

Whipstitch to
G between
arrows.

Do not
Whipstitch to
A; attach tail
here.

Whipstitch to
H between
arrows.

**F – Right Front
Inner Leg**
(cut 1 from stiff)
13 x 16 holes

Overcast

COLOR KEY: Country Santa

Ribbon floss			AMOUNT
■ Red			1 yd.
▨ Black			1/4 yd.
■ Royal			1/4 yd.
▨ White			1/4 yd.

Bumples™ or textured yarn			AMOUNT
▨ White			16 yds.

Worsted-weight	Nylon Plus™	Need-loft®	YARN AMOUNT
▨ White	#01	#41	45 yds.
■ Black	#02	#00	38 yds.
□ Dk. Red	#20	#01	27 yds.
▨ Green	#58	#28	12 yds.
▨ Dusty Rose	#52	#06	10 yds.
▨ Maple	#35	#13	6 yds.
▨ Peach	#46	#47	5 yds.
▨ Red	#19	#02	4 yds.
▨ Eggshell	#24	#39	3 yds.
▨ Gray	#23	#38	3 yds.
▨ Dk. Brown	#36	#15	1 yd.
▨ Flesh	#14	#56	1 yd.
■ Pink	#11	#07	1 yd.
▨ Straw	#41	#19	1 yd.

STITCH KEY:
— Backstitch/Straight Stitch
● French Knot
☞ Lark's Head Knot
✦ Cow Ear Attachment
✦ Chicken Wing Attachment

H – Cow Rear Piece
(cut 1)
14 x 14 holes

Whipstitch to B.
Whipstitch to A.

M – Tree
(cut 2)
21 x 21 holes

Whipstitch between arrows.

Country Santa Assembly Diagram
(Pieces are shown in different colors for contrast.)

Step 3:
With matching colors, tack each K and L piece to cow side as indicated.

Step 1:
Holding A, C and E pieces wrong sides together at matching edges, with matching colors, Whipstitch together through all thicknesses.

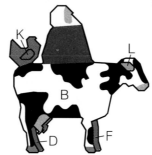

Step 2:
Holding B, D and F pieces wrong sides together at matching edges, with matching colors, Whipstitch together through all thicknesses.

Step 4:
Glue knotted end of tail to wrong side of one cow side at indicated area; trim tail tassel to 1 1/2".

Step 5:
With matching colors (**NOTE:** Use remaining yarn hair strands for Santa hair Whipstitch area), Whipstitch A, B, G and H pieces together as indicated.

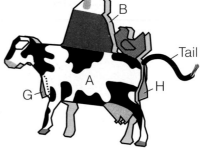

Step 6:
With matching colors, Whipstitch remaining edges of A and B pieces together; Overcast unfinished edges of G and H pieces.

G – Cow Chest Piece
(cut 1)
15 x 15 holes

Whipstitch to B.
Whipstitch to A.

J – Santa Arm
(cut 2)
15 x 17 holes

Nesting Santas

SIZE: Large Santa is 4¼" across x 4" tall; Medium Santa is 3¼" across x 2¾" tall; Small Santa is 2⅜" across x 2" tall.

SKILL LEVEL: Average

MATERIALS: One 9½" and two 6" plastic canvas radial circles; One each gold 5-, 10- and 15-mm jingle bells; Invisible thread; #3 pearl cotton or six-strand embroidery floss (for amount see Color Key); Worsted-weight or plastic canvas yarn (for amounts see Color Key).

CUTTING INSTRUCTIONS:

NOTE: Cut each circle in half, leaving

Ring in the season when you display this trio of Santas.

straight bar running across center.

A: For large Santa, cut away outer three rows of holes from one 9½" circle.

B: For medium Santa, use one 6" circle.

C: For small Santa, cut away outer five rows of holes from one 6" circle.

STITCHING INSTRUCTIONS:

1: Using colors and stitches indicated, work pieces according to graphs; fill in uncoded areas using red and Continental Stitch. Using yarn and pearl cotton or six strands floss in colors and embroidery stitches indicated, embroider detail as indicated on graphs.

2: For each Santa, holding straight edge together forming a cone, with matching colors, Whipstitch together; with white, Overcast bottom edge.

3: With invisible thread, sew 15-mm to Large, 10-mm to Medium and 5-mm jingle bell to Small Santa as shown in photo.❋

– Designed by Cherie Marie Leck

A – Large Santa
(cut 1 from 9½" circle)

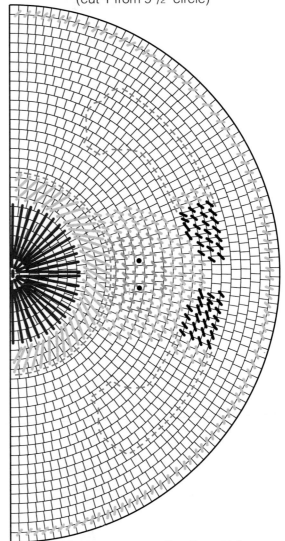

B – Medium Santa
(cut 1 from 6" circle)

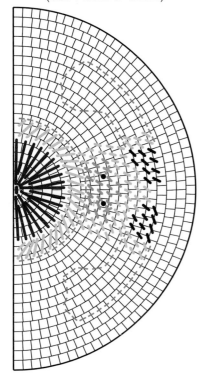

C – Small Santa
(cut 1 from 6" circle)

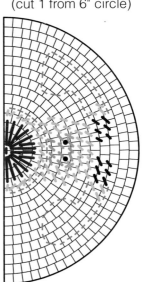

COLOR KEY: Nesting Santas

#3 pearl cotton			AMOUNT
Black			10 yds.

Worsted-weight	Nylon Plus™	Need-loft®	YARN AMOUNT
Dk. Red	#20	#01	34 yds.
White	#01	#41	13 yds.
Black	#02	#00	3 yds.
Coral	–	#65	2 yds.
Watermelon	#54	#55	1 yd.

STITCH KEY:

– Backstitch/Straight Stitch

● French Knot

Santa's Place Mat

SIZE: 10" x 13"

SKILL LEVEL: Easy

MATERIALS: One sheet of 7-count plastic canvas; #3 pearl cotton or six-strand embroidery floss (for amounts see Color Key); Worsted-weight or plastic canvas yarn (for amounts see Color Key).

CUTTING INSTRUCTIONS:

A: For Place Mat, cut one according to graph.

STITCHING INSTRUCTIONS:

1: Using colors and stitches indicated, work according to graph; fill in uncoded areas using tangerine and Continental Stitch. With eggshell,

Overcast unfinished edges.

2: Using pearl cotton or six strands floss in colors indicated and French Knot, embroider detail as indicated on graph.❄

– Designed by Michele Wilcox

COLOR KEY: Santa's Place Mat

#3 pearl cotton			AMOUNT
Black			1/2 yd.
Red			1/4 yd.
Worsted-weight	**Nylon Plus™**	**Need-loft®**	**YARN AMOUNT**
Green	#58	#28	35 yds.
Tangerine	#15	#11	30 yds.
White	#01	#41	16 yds.
Eggshell	#24	#39	12 yds.
Crimson	#53	#42	10 yds.
Coral	–	#65	1 yd.

STITCH KEY:

- • French Knot

A – Place Mat (cut 1) 66 x 86 holes

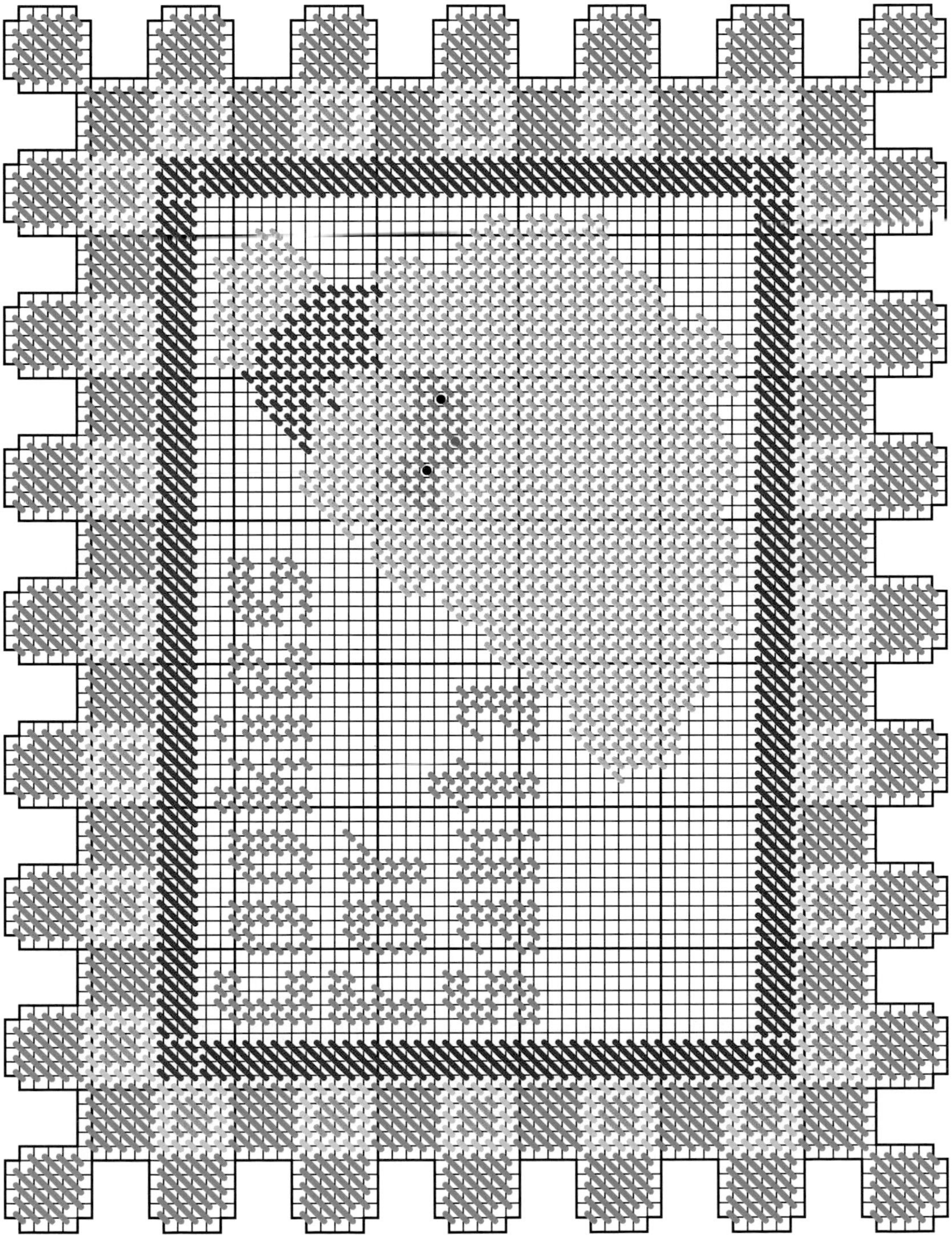

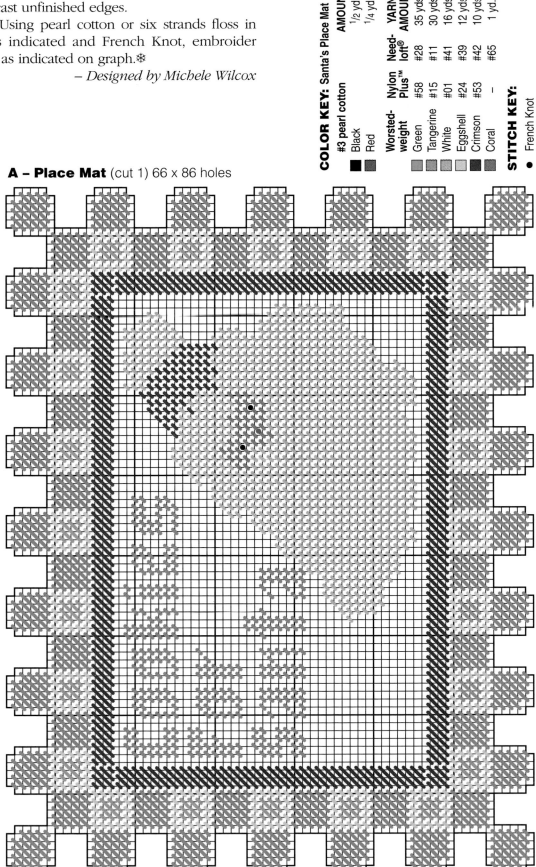

Winter Wizard

SIZE: 8½" across x 12⅝" tall.

SKILL LEVEL: Challenging

MATERIALS: Three sheets of 7-count plastic canvas; Two 4-mm black half-round beads; Forty-four 5-mm clear faceted half-round acrylic stones; 1½ yds. white 1" fur ribbon or ⅛ yd. white fur fabric; ¼ yd. white ⅛" satin ribbon; Two ½" white heart pony beads with ⅛" hole; One 4½" white lollipop stick; Craft glue or glue gun; Pearlized cord (for amount see Color Key on page 29); Worsted-weight or plastic canvas yarn (for amounts see Color Key).

CUTTING INSTRUCTIONS:

NOTE: Graphs on page 29.

A: For body pieces, cut six according to graph.

B: For collar, cut one according to graph.

C: For arms, cut two according to graph.

D: For hat, cut one according to graph.

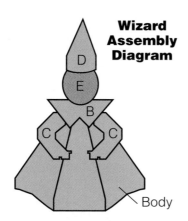

Wizard Assembly Diagram

Body

Santa's Hints

STRAIGHT PINS – Over the years, I've found that many decorative items can be hung with regular straight pins used for sewing. I use them just like nails and lightly tap them with a small hammer to drive them into the wall. Sometimes it takes two pins rather than one nail, but when Mrs. Claus and I take the decorations down, the pins leave virtually no marks on the wall.

E: For head, cut one according to graph.

F: For base, cut one according to graph.

STITCHING INSTRUCTIONS:

NOTES: F piece is not worked. Use Continental Stitch throughout.

1: Using orchid, work E, and work C pieces (one on opposite side of canvas) according to graph; fill in uncoded areas of C pieces, and work A, B and D pieces using pearl/white. With matching colors, Overcast edges of B and C pieces.

2: With pearl/white, Whipstitch A pieces together and to F as indicated on graphs, forming body. Whipstitch short ends of D together as indicated; Overcast unfinished edges of hat.

3: Using plum and Backstitch, embroider mouth on E as indicated. With orchid, Whipstitch X edges of E together, then Whipstitch short ends together as indicated.

4: Glue body, collar, arms, head and hat together according to Wizard Assembly Diagram. Glue black beads to head for eyes and stones (one will be left for wand) to Wizard as indicated.

NOTE: Cut one 1" x 26" piece for body bottom trim, three ½" x 7" pieces for hat and collar trim, two ½" x 1¼" pieces for arm cuff trim and one ½" x 1" piece of fur for beard; cut four thin 1" strips of fur for hair, mustache and wand.

5: Glue bottom trim to bottom edge of body, one ½" x 7" piece around base of hat and remaining ½" x 7" pieces to each side of collar as shown. Glue one cuff trim to each arm above hand, beard under mouth, one thin strip above mouth for mustache and remaining thin strips to head for hair.

6: For wand, glue one heart bead to each end of lollipop stick; glue remaining 1" thin strip of fur below one heart around stick. Tie ribbon into a small bow with long tails; glue bow to fur end of wand. Glue remaining 5-mm stone to bow. Slip wand between body and arm as shown and glue to secure.❈

– Designed by Robin Will

Add a touch of Yuletide enchantment with a snowy, fur-trimmed Santa centerpiece or tree topper. Like Merlin of old, he sprinkles the magic of Christmas wishes like stardust.

Tyrolean Match Holder

SIZE: 4¼" x 8" x 11⅞" tall.

SKILL LEVEL: Average

MATERIALS: Two sheets of 7-count plastic canvas; Bundle of 11½"-long fireplace matches; Black and red six-strand embroidery floss; 1" cardboard; Small zip-close bag filled with gravel or other weighting material; #3 pearl cotton or six-strand embroidery floss (for amounts see Color Key on page 28); Worsted-weight or plastic canvas yarn (for amounts see Color Key).

CUTTING INSTRUCTIONS:

NOTE: Graphs on page 28.

A: For support sides, cut four 7 x 50 holes.

B: For support top and bottom, cut two (one for top and one for bottom) 7 x 7 holes (no graph).

C: For match loop, cut one 3 x 39 holes.

D: For ice, cut one according to graph.

E: For base top and bottom, cut two (one for top and one for bottom) 27 x 44 holes (no graph).

F: For base sides, cut two 6 x 44 holes and two 6 x 27 holes (no graphs).

G: For jacket, cut one according to graph.

H: For sleeves, cut two according to graph.

I: For legs, cut one according to graph.

J: For face, cut one according to graph.

K: For hat trim and beard, cut one according to graph.

L: For mustache pieces, cut two according to graph.

M: For sack, cut one according to graph.

STITCHING INSTRUCTIONS:

1: Using colors and stitches indicated, work A, C, G-K (one H on opposite side of canvas) and M pieces according to graphs; fill in uncoded areas of J using lt. pink and Continental Stitch. Using white and Continental Stitch, work B and D pieces; using mint and Continental Stitch, work E and F pieces. With mint for main jacket and sleeve color (see photo), dusty rose for sack, white for mustache pieces and with matching colors, Overcast unfinished edges of C, D and G-M (one L on opposite side of canvas) pieces.

2: Using colors and embroidery stitches indicated, embroider detail on G, H, J and K pieces as indicated on graphs. For sack tie, wrap remaining gold pearl cotton or floss around tapered end of sack three times and knot in front to secure.

3: With white, Whipstitch A and B pieces together; with mint, Whipstitch E and F pieces together, inserting weight before closing. (See Base & Support Assembly Diagram.)

4: Glue support, base, C and D pieces together as indicated and according to diagram. Glue G-M pieces together and to base and support as shown in photo.

NOTE: Cut black floss into one 1-yd. and one 12" length and red floss into one 12" length.

5: For tassel, wrap 1-yd. floss strand around cardboard. Tie black 12" strand tightly around loops at one end; cut loops at opposite end. Wrap red 12" strand tightly around all strands ⅛" from tie; secure ends under wraps. Trim ends to even. Glue tassel to tip of cap as shown. ✲

– Designed by Celia Lange Designs

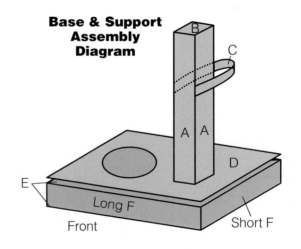

Base & Support Assembly Diagram

B

C

A A

D

E

Long F

Front

Short F

Invite an old world Santa from the mountains of Europe to your hearth and home.

Tyrolean Match Holder

Instructions & photo on pages 26 & 27

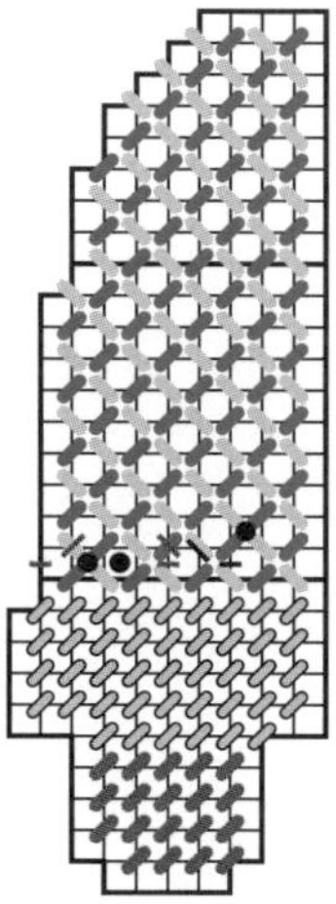

M – Sack
(cut 1) 20 x 27 holes

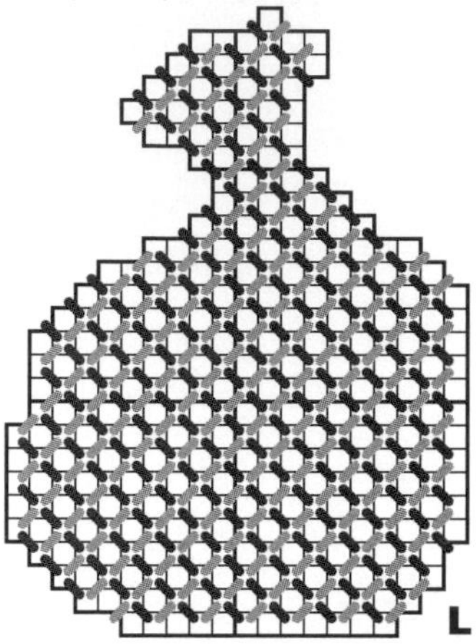

K – Hat Trim & Beard
(cut 1) 18 x 20 holes

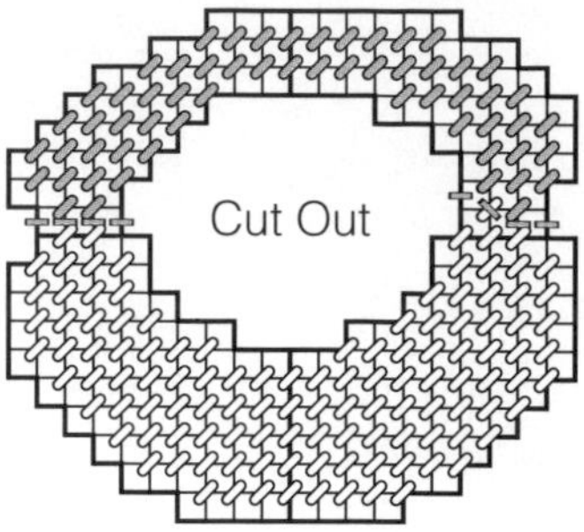

Cut Out

J – Face
(cut 1) 19 x 20 holes

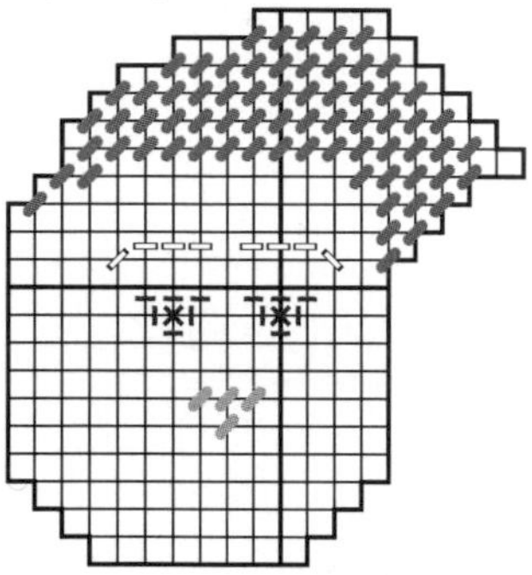

H – Sleeve
(cut 2)
10 x 28 holes

A – Support Side
(cut 4) 7 x 50 holes

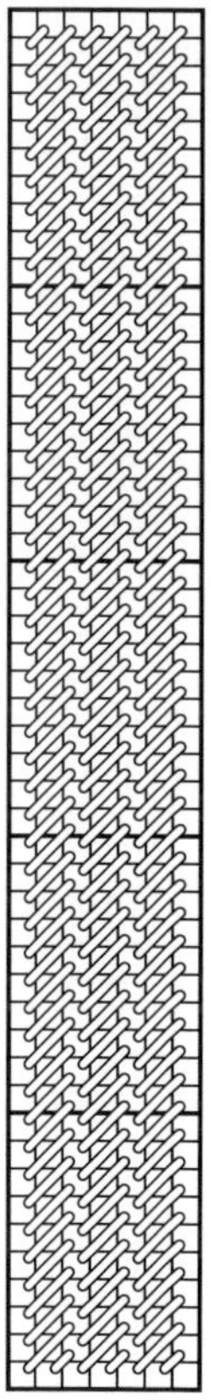

L – Mustache Piece
(cut 2)
3 x 4 holes

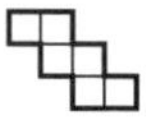

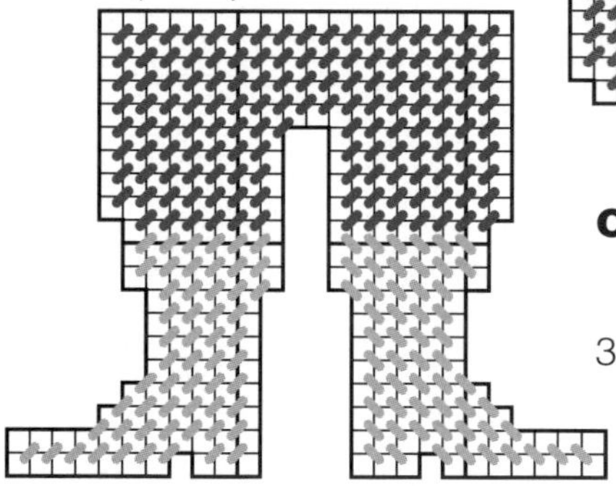

G – Jacket
(cut 1) 31 x 36 holes

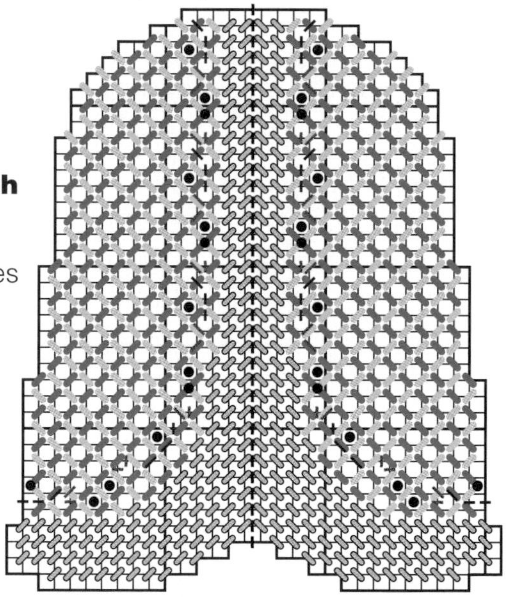

I – Legs
(cut 1) 20 x 26 holes

C – Match Loop
(cut 1)
3 x 39 holes

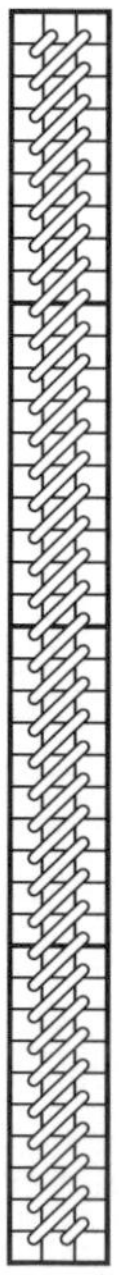

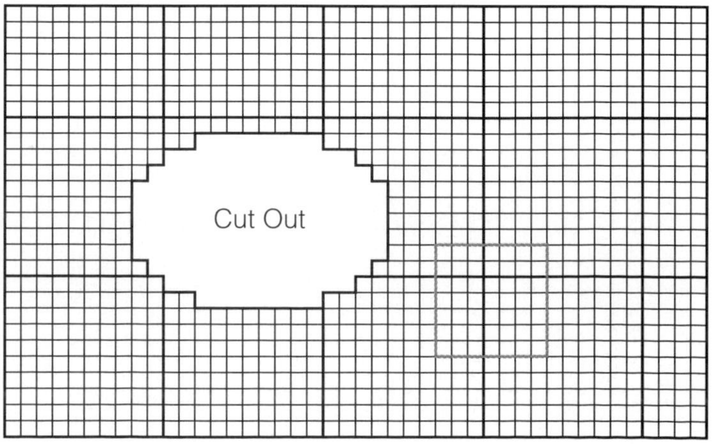

COLOR KEY: Tyrolean Match Holder

#3 pearl cotton or floss	AMOUNT
Brown	3 yds.
Gold	2$\frac{1}{2}$ yds.
Red	2 yds.
Black	1$\frac{1}{2}$ yds.

Worsted-weight	Nylon Plus™	Need-loft®	YARN AMOUNT
Mint	#30	#24	75 yds.
White	#01	#41	33 yds.
Beige	#43	#40	11 yds.
Lt. Green	#28	#26	10 yds.
Black	#02	#00	4 yds.
Dk. Brown	#36	#15	4 yds.
Dk. Red	#20	#01	3 yds.
Dusty Rose	#52	#06	3 yds.
Rose	#12	#05	3 yds.
Lt. Pink	#10	#08	2 yds.
Plum	#55	#59	$\frac{1}{4}$ yd.

STITCH KEY:
— Backstitch/Straight Stitch
● French Knot
☐ Support Placement

D – Ice (cut 1) 27 x 44 holes

Cut Out

Winter Wizard

Instructions & photo on pages 24 & 25

COLOR KEY: Winter Wizard

Pearlized cord			AMOUNT
☐ Pearl/White			80 yds.

Worsted-weight	Nylon Plus™	Need-loft®	YARN AMOUNT
▨ Orchid	#56	#44	10 yds.
■ Plum	#55	#59	¼ yd.

STITCH KEY:

- — Backstitch/Straight Stitch
- ○ Eye Placement
- ○ Stone Placement
- ○ Stone Placement (for front body piece only)

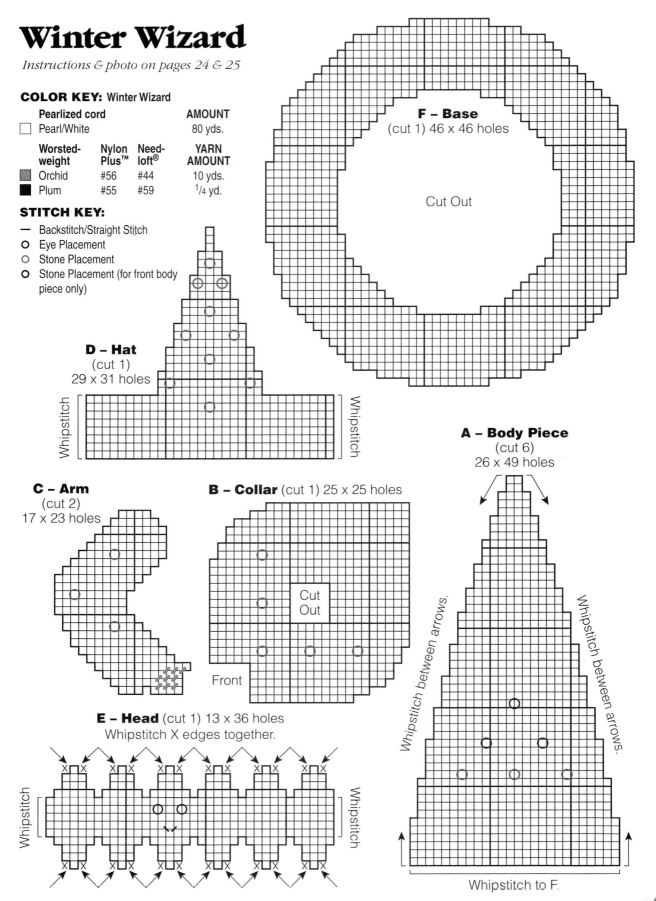

F – Base
(cut 1) 46 x 46 holes

Cut Out

D – Hat
(cut 1)
29 x 31 holes

Whipstitch

Whipstitch

A – Body Piece
(cut 6)
26 x 49 holes

Whipstitch between arrows.

Whipstitch between arrows.

Whipstitch to F.

C – Arm
(cut 2)
17 x 23 holes

B – Collar (cut 1) 25 x 25 holes

Cut Out

Front

E – Head (cut 1) 13 x 36 holes
Whipstitch X edges together.

Whipstitch

Whipstitch

Frosty Friends

Percival Penguin

SIZE: 3¾" x 5½" x 9½" tall.

SKILL LEVEL: Average

MATERIALS: 2½ sheets of 7-count plastic canvas; Two 15-mm oval wiggle eyes; One white ¾" pom-pom; ½" x 7½" strip of white artificial fur; Polyester fiberfill; 1½" evergreen wreath with bow; Craft glue or glue gun; Worsted-weight or plastic canvas yarn (for amounts see Color Key on page 37).

CUTTING INSTRUCTIONS:

NOTE: Graphs on page 37.

A: For front, cut one according to graph.

B: For sides, cut two according to graph.

C: For bottom, cut one according to graph.

D: For wings, cut two according to graph.

E: For hat curved side, cut two according to graph.

F: For hat straight side, cut one according to graph.

G: For feet, cut two according to graph.

H: For upper beak, cut one according to graph.

I: For lower beak, cut one according to graph.

STITCHING INSTRUCTIONS:

NOTE: C piece is not worked.

1: Using colors and stitches indicated, work A and G-I pieces according to graphs. Fill in uncoded areas of A, and work B and D pieces (one each on opposite side of canvas) using black and Continental Stitch. Using red and Continental Stitch, work E (one on opposite side of canvas) and F pieces. With matching colors, Overcast edges of G and D pieces as indicated on graph.

2: Whipstitch A-C pieces together as indicated and according to Body Assembly Diagram; Whipstitch E and F pieces together as indicated and according to Hat Assembly Diagram. With yellow, Whipstitch X edges of H together as indicated, and Whipstitch Y edges of I together as indicated; Overcast unfinished edges of beak pieces.

3: Glue white fur around rim and pom-pom to tip of hat; glue hat, eyes, beak, feet and wreath to body as shown in photo.❊

– Designed by Robin Will

Hat Assembly Diagram

Body Assembly Diagram

Step 1:
With black, Whipstitch A and B pieces together, attaching one D to each side as you work.

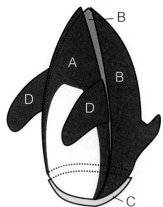

Step 2:
With matching colors, Whipstitch A and B pieces to C, stuffing body firmly with fiberfill before closing.

Tiny Tree Trimmings

GO TEAM! – Celebrate the world of sports with a tiny tree decorated with trinkets representing your favorite sport. Secure tree trunk in a new tennis shoe. Wrap matching shoe for gift and place under your full-size tree.

Wintery Wreath

SIZE: 10¼" x 11¾".

SKILL LEVEL: Average

MATERIALS: Three sheets of 7-count plastic canvas; 1½" orange chenille stem; 1¼ yds. iridescent clear metallic twist ribbon; Craft glue or glue gun; Metallic cord (for amount see Color Key); Pearlized metallic cord (for amount see Color Key); Worsted-weight or plastic canvas yarn (for amounts see Color Key).

CUTTING INSTRUCTIONS:

NOTES: Graphs continued on page 36.

Use 10-count for H and I and 7-count canvas for remaining pieces.

A: For wreath front and backing, cut two (one for front and one for backing) according to graph.

B: For snowman, cut one according to graph.

C: For snowman hat, cut one according to graph.

D: For tree #1, cut one according to graph.

E: For tree #2, cut one according to graph.

F: For deer, cut one according to graph.

G: For large snowflakes, cut three according to graph.

H: For small snowflakes, cut three according to G graph.

I: For birds #1 and #2, cut number indicated according to graphs.

STITCHING INSTRUCTIONS:

NOTE: One A piece is not worked for backing.

1: Using colors and stitches indicated, work one A for front and B-G pieces according to graphs. With white/silver cord for sled blade and with matching colors as shown in photo, Overcast edges of B-G pieces.

NOTE: Separate remaining yarn colors into 2-ply or nylon plastic canvas yarn into 1-ply strands.

2: Using 2-ply (or 1-ply) colors and stitches indicated, work H and I pieces according to graphs; with tangerine for beaks and with matching colors, Overcast edges.

3: Using pearlized cord and Straight Stitch, embroider G and H pieces as indicated on graphs. Using 2-ply (or 1-ply) colors and embroidery stitches indicated, embroider detail on B, F and I pieces as indicated.

4: Holding backing A to wrong side of front, with pearlized cord, Whipstitch together.

5: Bend orange chenille stem in half and glue over edge of snowman's face for nose as shown in photo. Glue trees to back and remaining pieces together and to front of wreath as desired or as shown.

6: Tie metallic twist ribbon into a multi-loop bow; trim ends as desired. Glue bow to wreath as shown. Hang as desired.❄

– Designed by Robin Petrina

COLOR KEY: Wintery Wreath

Metallic cord			AMOUNT
White/Silver			5 yds.

Pearlized cord			AMOUNT
Blue			3 yds.

Worsted-weight	Nylon Plus™	Need-loft®	YARN AMOUNT
Lt. Blue	#05	#36	28 yds.
Green	#58	#28	9 yds.
White	#01	#41	8 yds.
Dk. Green	#31	#27	7 yds.
Black	#02	#00	3 yds.
Camel	#34	#43	3 yds.
Royal	#09	#32	2½ yds.
Red	#19	#02	2 yds.
Eggshell	#24	#39	¼ yd.
Tangerine	#15	#11	¼ yd.

STITCH KEY:
- — Backstitch/Straight Stitch
- ● French Knot

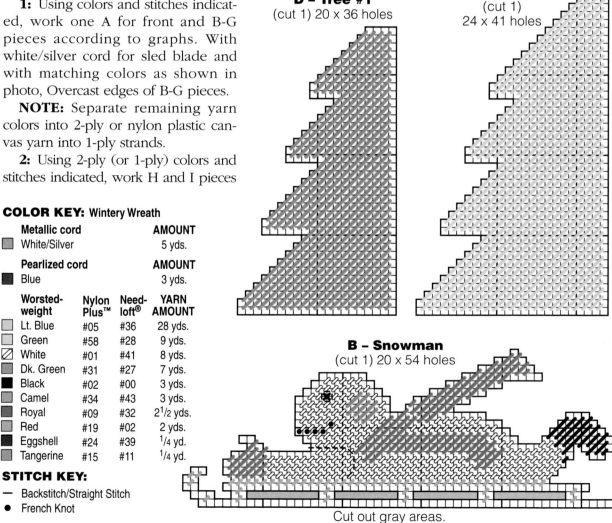

D – Tree #1
(cut 1) 20 x 36 holes

E – Tree #2
(cut 1)
24 x 41 holes

B – Snowman
(cut 1) 20 x 54 holes

Cut out gray areas.

Wintery Wreath

Instructions & photo on pages 34 & 35

COLOR KEY: Wintery Wreath

Metallic cord			AMOUNT
White/Silver			5 yds.
Pearlized cord			**AMOUNT**
Blue			3 yds.

Worsted-weight	Nylon Plus™	Need-loft®	YARN AMOUNT
Lt. Blue	#05	#36	28 yds.
Green	#58	#28	9 yds.
White	#01	#41	8 yds.
Dk. Green	#31	#27	7 yds.
Black	#02	#00	3 yds.
Camel	#34	#43	3 yds.
Royal	#09	#32	2$\frac{1}{2}$ yds.
Red	#19	#02	2 yds.
Eggshell	#24	#39	$\frac{1}{4}$ yd.
Tangerine	#15	#11	$\frac{1}{4}$ yd.

STITCH KEY:

— Backstitch/Straight Stitch
• French Knot

G – Large Snowflake
(cut 3)
13 x 13 holes

H – Small Snowflake
(cut 3 from 10-count)
13 x 13 holes

F – Deer
(cut 1)
17 x 17 holes

C – Snowman Hat
(cut 1) 8 x 15 holes

A – Wreath Front & Backing
(cut 1 each) 68 x 68 holes

I – Bird #1
(cut 1 from 10-count)
8 x 9 holes

Cut Out

I – Bird #2
(cut 2 from 10-count)
8 x 9 holes

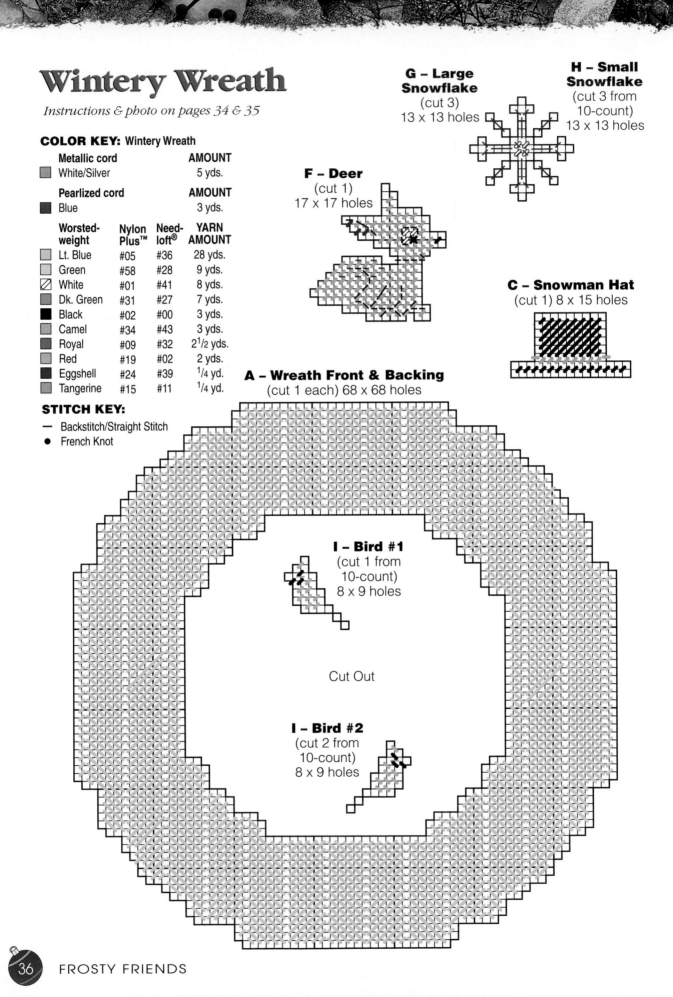

Percival Penguin

Instructions & photo on pages 32 & 33

H – Upper Beak
(cut 1)
9 x 12 holes

Whipstitch X edges together.

F – Hat Straight Side
(cut 1) 14 x 17 holes

Whipstitch to one E.

Whipstitch to one E.

G – Foot
(cut 2)
10 x 11 holes

I – Lower Beak
(cut 1)
5 x 11 holes

Whipstitch Y edges together.

B – Side
(cut 2) 31 x 53 holes

Whipstitch to A between purple arrows.

Whipstitch to one B between green arrows.

Whipstitch to C.

D – Wing
(cut 2)
14 x 18 holes

Overcast between arrows.

A – Front
(cut 1) 24 x 53 holes

Whipstitch to one B between purple arrows.

Whipstitch to one B between purple arrows.

Whipstitch to C.

C – Bottom
(cut 1) 17 x 19 holes

Whipstitch to one B.

Whipstitch to one B.

Whipstitch to A.

E – Hat Curved Side
(cut 2) 14 x 18 holes

Whipstitch to F.

Whipstitch to one E between arrows.

COLOR KEY: Percival Penguin

	Worsted-weight	Nylon Plus™	Need-loft®	YARN AMOUNT
	Black	#02	#00	38 yds.
	Red	#19	#02	8 yds.
	White	#01	#41	8 yds.
	Yellow	#26	#57	7 yds.

STITCH KEY:
☐ Wing Attachment

Spell out your passion for winter's gift in a cheerful block arrangement.

I Love Snow

SIZE: 1⅞" x 7½" x 6¾" tall.

SKILL LEVEL: Average

MATERIALS: Two sheets of 7-count plastic canvas; Craft glue or glue gun; 1/16" metallic ribbon (for amounts see Color Key on page 43); Medium metallic braid or metallic cord (for amounts see Color Key); Sport-weight yarn (for amount see Color Key); Worsted-weight or plastic canvas yarn (for amounts see Color Key).

CUTTING INSTRUCTIONS:

NOTE: Graphs on page 43.

A: For large cube pieces, cut thirty-six 11 x 11 holes.

B: For small box sides, cut two 11 x 11 holes (no graphs).

C: For small box ends, cut four 5 x 11 holes (no graph).

D: For snowman hat, cut one according to graph.

E: For snowman head, cut one according to graph.

F: For snowman upper body, cut one according to graph.

G: For snowman lower body, cut one according to graph.

H: For snowman arms, cut two according to graph.

I: For snowman vest, cut one according to graph.

STITCHING INSTRUCTIONS:

1: Using colors and stitches indicated, work one A according to Large Cube Heart Piece graph, D, E and I pieces according to graphs. *Continued on page 43*

Continued on page 43

Mini Frosty Basket

SIZE: 2⅞" square x 5¾" tall, including handle.

SKILL LEVEL: Easy

MATERIALS: One sheet of 7-count plastic canvas; Craft glue or glue gun; #3 pearl cotton or six-strand embroidery floss (for amount see Color Key); Worsted-weight or plastic canvas yarn (for amounts see Color Key).

CUTTING INSTRUCTIONS:

A: For sides, cut four 18 x 18 holes.

B: For bottom, cut one 18 x 18 holes (no graph).

C: For handle, cut one 3 x 70 holes (no graph).

STITCHING INSTRUCTIONS:

1: Using colors indicated and Continental Stitch, work A pieces according to graph. Using dusty blue and Continental Stitch, work B and C pieces. With dusty blue, Overcast edges of C.

2: Using pearl cotton or six strands floss and French Knot, embroider facial detail as indicated on graph.

3: With dusty blue, Whipstitch A and B pieces together, forming Basket; Overcast unfinished edges. Glue ends of handle to inside of Basket as shown in photo.❄

– Designed by Michele Wilcox

A – Side
(cut 4)
18 x 18 holes

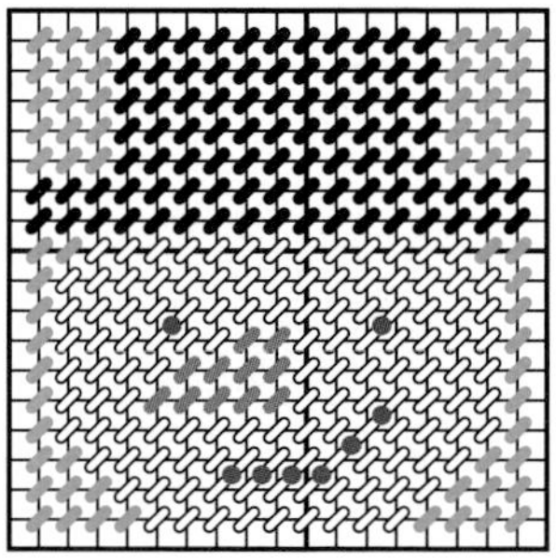

COLOR KEY: Mini Frosty Basket

	#3 pearl cotton or floss			AMOUNT
■	Black			3 yds.
	Worsted-weight	**Nylon Plus™**	**Need-loft®**	**YARN AMOUNT**
■	Dusty Blue	#38	#34	20 yds.
▨	White	#01	#41	9 yds.
■	Black	#02	#00	5 yds.
■	Pumpkin	#50	#12	2 yds.

STITCH KEY:

● French Knot

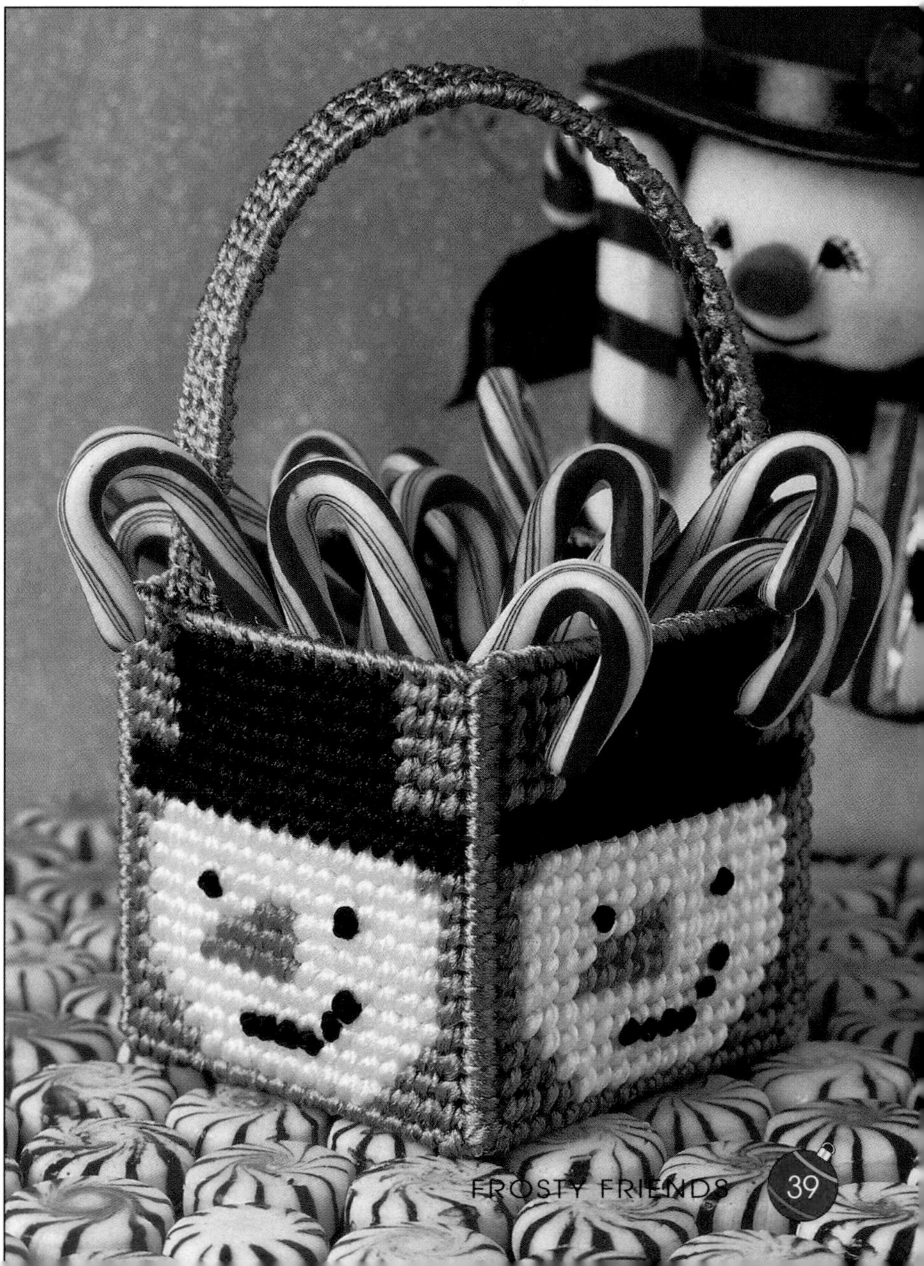

Penguin Party

SIZE: Bowl is 9½" across x 5" tall, including motifs; Doorstop is 2¾" x 8¾" x 5½" tall, including motifs.

SKILL LEVEL: Average

MATERIALS: One 12" x 18" or larger sheet and two standard-size sheets of 7-count plastic canvas; One 9½" plastic canvas radial circle; 2½" x 3½" x 8" brick or zip-close bag filled with gravel or other weighting material; 12 assorted color ½" glitter pom-poms; One 3½" x 28" piece of white felt (optional); Craft glue or glue gun; Worsted-weight or plastic canvas yarn (for amounts see Color Key).

CUTTING INSTRUCTIONS:

NOTES: Graphs continued on page 42.

Use large sheet for A pieces.

A: For Bowl side pieces, cut one 21 x 120 holes and one 21 x 73 holes (no graphs).

B: For Bowl bottom, use 9½" plastic canvas circle (no graph).

C: For Doorstop sides, cut two 26 x 56 holes (no graph).

D: For Doorstop ends, cut two 16 x 26 holes (no graph).

E: For Doorstop top and bottom, cut two (one for top and one for bottom) 16 x 56 holes (no graph).

F: For penguins #1-#7, cut number indicated according to graphs.

G: For trees, cut four according to graph.

STITCHING INSTRUCTIONS:

NOTE: B piece is not worked.

1: Using colors and stitches indicated, work A and C-G pieces according to graphs and Stitch Pattern Guide; fill in uncoded areas of F pieces using white and Continental Stitch. With matching colors, Overcast edges of F and G pieces.

2: Using colors and embroidery stitches indicated, embroider detail on F pieces as indicated on graphs.

3: With lt. blue, Whipstitch A and B pieces together according to Bowl Assembly Diagram; Overcast unfinished edges. If desired, line inside of bowl with felt.

4: For Doorstop, holding C-E pieces wrong sides together, with lt. blue; Whipstitch together, inserting weight before closing.

5: Glue pom-poms to F pieces as indicated; glue penguins and trees around Bowl and to one side of Doorstop as desired or as shown in photo.❈

– Designed by Cherie Marie Leck

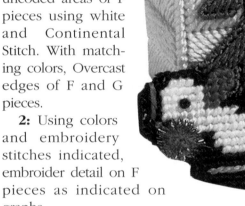

G – Tree
(cut 4)
25 x 33 holes

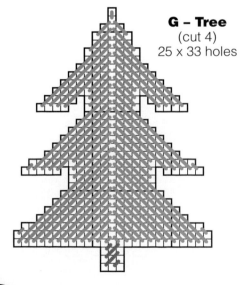

COLOR KEY: Penguin Party

Worsted-weight	Nylon Plus™	Need-loft®	YARN AMOUNT
Lt. Blue	#05	#36	2½ oz.
Black	#02	#00	18 yds.
Dk. Green	#31	#27	16 yds.
White	#01	#41	11 yds.
Dk. Orange	#18	#52	5 yds.
Gray	#23	#38	3 yds.
Dk. Red	#20	#01	2 yds.
Maple	#35	#13	2 yds.

STITCH KEY:

— Backstitch/Straight Stitch
● French Knot
○ Pom-Pom Placement

Bowl Assembly Diagram

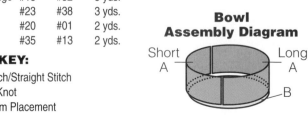

Invite these playful pals to your next holiday bash.

Penguin Party

Instructions & photo on pages 40 & 41

Bowl & Doorstop Stitch Pattern Guide

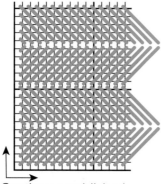

Continue established pattern up and across each entire piece.

F – Penguin #2
(cut 2)
20 x 22 holes

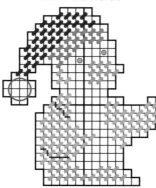

F – Penguin #1
(cut 2)
30 x 31 holes

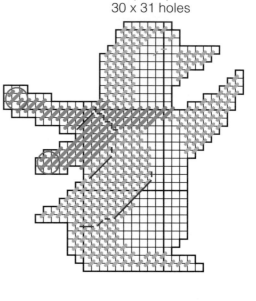

F – Penguin #3
(cut 2)
17 x 24 holes

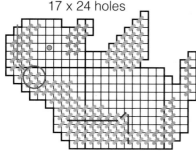

F – Penguin #4
(cut 1) 21 x 24 holes

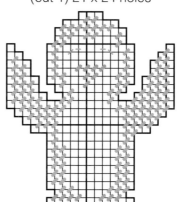

F – Penguin #5
(cut 1)
17 x 23 holes

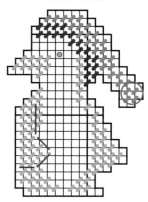

F – Penguin #6
(cut 1)
17 x 23 holes

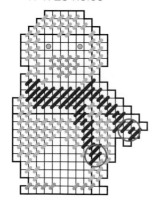

F – Penguin #7
(cut 1)
14 x 22 holes

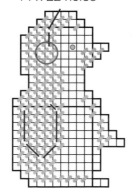

COLOR KEY: Penguin Party

	Worsted-weight	Nylon Plus™	Need-loft®	YARN AMOUNT
	Lt. Blue	#05	#36	2¹/₂ oz.
	Black	#02	#00	18 yds.
	Dk. Green	#31	#27	16 yds.
	White	#01	#41	11 yds.
	Dk. Orange	#18	#52	5 yds.
	Gray	#23	#38	3 yds.
	Dk. Red	#20	#01	2 yds.
	Maple	#35	#13	2 yds.

STITCH KEY:

— Backstitch/Straight Stitch
● French Knot
○ Pom-Pom Placement

I Love Snow

Continued from page 38

Fill in uncoded areas of worked A and work remaining A pieces, B, C and E-H (one H on opposite side of canvas) pieces using white and Continental Stitch. With black for hat and with matching colors, Overcast edges of D-I pieces.

2: Using colors and embroidery stitches indicated, embroider detail on five A pieces (follow one of each letter graph), D, E and I pieces as indicated on graphs.

3: For each large cube (make 6), holding five solid A pieces and one embroidered or motif-stitched A piece wrong sides together, with white, Whipstitch together. For small box, with white, Whipstitch B and C pieces together.

4: Glue cubes and box together according to Cubes Assembly Diagram. Glue D-I pieces together as shown in photo, forming snowman; glue snowman to small box as shown.❄

– Designed by Celia Lange Designs

A – Large Cube "I" Piece
(cut 1)
11 x 11 holes

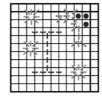

A – Large Cube "S" Piece
(cut 1)
11 x 11 holes

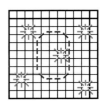

A – Large Cube "Heart" Piece
(cut 1)
11 x 11 holes

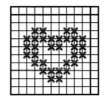

A – Large Cube "O" Piece
(cut 1)
11 x 11 holes

A – Large Cube "N" Piece
(cut 1)
11 x 11 holes

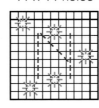

F – Snowman Upper Body
(cut 1)
10 x 10 holes

D – Snowman Hat
(cut 1) 7 x 10 holes

H – Snowman Arm
(cut 2)
8 x 10 holes

A – Large Cube "W" Piece
(cut 1)
11 x 11 holes

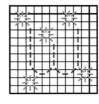

G – Snowman Lower Body
(cut 1) 13 x 13 holes

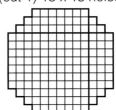

E – Snowman Head
(cut 1)
8 x 8 holes

COLOR KEY: I Love Snow

1/16" metallic ribbon	AMOUNT
■ Blue	1 yd.
■ Green	1/4 yd.
■ Red	1/4 yd.

Med. metallic braid or cord	AMOUNT
■ White/Blue	2 yds.
■ Gold	1/4 yd.

Sport-weight	YARN AMOUNT
□ White	65 yds.

Worsted-weight	Nylon Plus™	Need-loft®	YARN AMOUNT
■ Green	#58	#28	2 yds.
■ Black	#02	#00	1 1/2 yds.
■ Dk. Red	#20	#01	1 yd.
■ Orange	#17	#58	1/4 yd.

STITCH KEY:
— Backstitch/Straight Stitch
● French Knot

I – Snowman Vest
(cut 1) 8 x 11 holes

Cubes Assembly Diagram

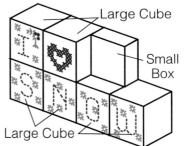

Large Cube

Small Box

Large Cube

Christmas Wall Hanging

SIZE: 11¼" x 16".

SKILL LEVEL: Average

MATERIALS: Four sheets of 7-count plastic canvas; Sewing needle; Three black 3-mm beads; Six rose ½" four-hole buttons; Craft glue or glue gun; #3 pearl cotton or six-strand embroidery floss (for amount see Color Key); Worsted-weight or plastic canvas yarn (for amounts see Color Key).

CUTTING INSTRUCTIONS:

NOTE: Graphs continued on page 49.

A: For base front and backing, use two (one for front and one for backing) 70- x 90-hole sheets.

B: For trees, cut two according to graph.

C: For snowman, cut one according to graph.

D: For broom, cut one according to graph.

E: For letter blocks, cut fourteen 10 x 10 holes.

STITCHING INSTRUCTIONS:

1: Using colors and stitches indicated, work one A for front and B-E pieces (work letters on each block to spell "Merry Christmas") according to graphs and stitch pattern guide; fill in un-coded areas of C using eggshell and Continental Stitch. With dk. red for letter blocks and with matching colors, Overcast edges of B-E pieces.

2: Using pearl cotton or six strands floss and Backstitch, embroider facial detail on C as indicated on graph; sew beads and buttons to C as indicated.

3: Holding backing A to wrong side of front, with crimson, Whipstitch together.

4: Glue B-E pieces to A as desired or as shown in photo. Hang as desired.✳

– Designed by Michele Wilcox

C – Snowman
(cut 1) 42 x 60 holes

COLOR KEY: Christmas Wall Hanging

#3 pearl cotton or floss			AMOUNT
■ Black			2 yds.

Worsted-weight	Nylon Plus™	Need-loft®	YARN AMOUNT
▨ Sail Blue	#04	#35	70 yds.
□ Eggshell	#24	#39	40 yds.
▨ Forest	#32	#29	40 yds.
■ Crimson	#53	#42	16 yds.
□ Dk. Red	#20	#01	14 yds.
▨ Camel	#34	#43	4 yds.
▨ Maple	#35	#13	4 yds.
▨ Tangerine	#15	#11	4 yds.
▨ Black	#02	#00	2 yds.
▨ Dk. Green	#31	#27	1 yd.

STITCH KEY:
- □ Letter Placement
- ○ Bead Attachment
- ○ Button Attachment

Warm Winter Friends

SIZE: 6" x 10" x 11" tall.

SKILL LEVEL: Average

MATERIALS: Four sheets of 7-count plastic canvas; Seven black 5-mm half-round beads; Two black 4-mm half-round beads; One white ¼" pom-pom; One pink 3-mm pom-pom; Polyester fiberfill; Craft glue or glue gun; Worsted-weight or plastic canvas yarn (for amounts see Color Key).

COLOR KEY: Warm Winter Friends

	Worsted-weight	Nylon Plus™	Need-loft®	YARN AMOUNT
	White	#01	#41	40 yds.
	Royal	#09	#32	12 yds.
	Black	#02	#00	10 yds.
	Maple	#35	#13	7 yds.
	Eggshell	#24	#39	4 yds.
	Dk. Green	#31	#27	1 yd.
	Orange	#17	#58	1 yd.
	Red	#19	#02	½ yd.

STITCH KEY:

— Backstitch/Straight Stitch

▲ Fringe Attachment

O Bead Placement

CUTTING INSTRUCTIONS:

NOTE: Graphs continued on pages 48 & 49.

A: For snowman front and back, cut two (one for front and one for back) according to graph.

B: For snowman bottom, cut one according to graph.

C: For snowman nose, cut one according to graph.

D: For snowman hat, cut one 12 x 40 holes.

E: For snowman hat top, cut one according to graph.

F: For snowman hat brim, cut one according to graph.

G: For snowman scarf front, cut one according to graph.

H: For snowman scarf back, cut one according to graph.

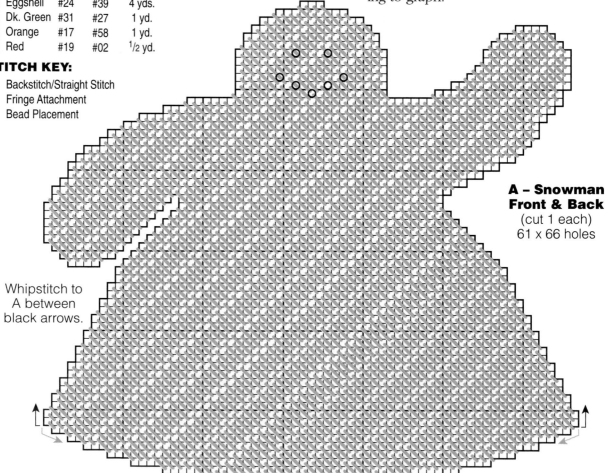

Whipstitch to A between black arrows.

A – Snowman Front & Back
(cut 1 each)
61 x 66 holes

Whipstitch to B between blue arrows.

Send this dapper gentleman and his forest companions out on the porch to welcome guests.

I: For broom, cut one according to graph.

J: For bird, cut one according to graph.

K: For rabbit, cut one according to graph.

L: For rabbit scarf, cut one according to graph.

STITCHING INSTRUCTIONS:

NOTE: Use a doubled strand of yarn for Long Stitches on D.

1: Using colors and stitches indicated, work A (one on opposite side of canvas) and B-L pieces according to graphs. With matching colors, Overcast edges of C and G-L pieces.

NOTE: Separate ¼ yd. black into 2-ply or nylon plastic canvas yarn into 1-ply strands.

2: Using 2-ply (or 1-ply) black and Backstitch, embroider wing on J as indicated on graph.

3: With white, Whipstitch A and B pieces together as indicated and according to Snowman Assembly Diagram, stuffing with fiberfill before closing. With black, Whipstitch ends of D together as indicated. Whipstitch D-F pieces together according to Hat Assembly Diagram; Overcast unfinished edges of brim.

NOTE: Cut fourteen 4" lengths of royal.

4: For scarf fringe, using a Lark's Head Knot, attach one 4" strand to each ▲ hole on G as indicated; trim ends to even.

5: Glue large beads and nose to front A as indicated (see photo) and one small bead to each J and K as indicated. Glue white pom-pom to top of bird, and pink pom-pom and rabbit scarf to rabbit as shown in photo. Glue H to back of snowman and hat, broom, scarf front and rabbit to front of snowman as shown. Glue bird to hat as shown.❋

– Designed by Robin Will

Warm Winter Friends

Instructions & photo on pages 46 & 47

F – Snowman Hat Brim
(cut 1) 15 x 25 holes

Cut Out

**G – Snowman
Scarf Front**
(cut 1) 25 x 36 holes

**H – Snowman
Scarf Back**
(cut 1) 9 x 21 holes

E – Snowman Hat Top
(cut 1) 7 x 19 holes

J – Bird
(cut 1)
10 x 10 holes

I – Broom
(cut 1)
52 x 52 holes

Snowman Assembly Diagram
(underside view)

A

A

B

**C – Snowman
Nose**
(cut 1)
3 x 3 holes

Glue to
front.

K – Rabbit
(cut 1)
12 x 16 holes

B – Snowman Bottom
(cut 1) 42 x 42 holes

COLOR KEY: Warm Winter Friends

	Worsted-weight	Nylon Plus™	Need-loft®	YARN AMOUNT
	White	#01	#41	40 yds.
	Royal	#09	#32	12 yds.
	Black	#02	#00	10 yds.
	Maple	#35	#13	7 yds.
	Eggshell	#24	#39	4 yds.
	Dk. Green	#31	#27	1 yd.
	Orange	#17	#58	1 yd.
	Red	#19	#02	1/2 yd.

STITCH KEY:
— Backstitch/Straight Stitch
▲ Fringe Attachment
O Bead Placement

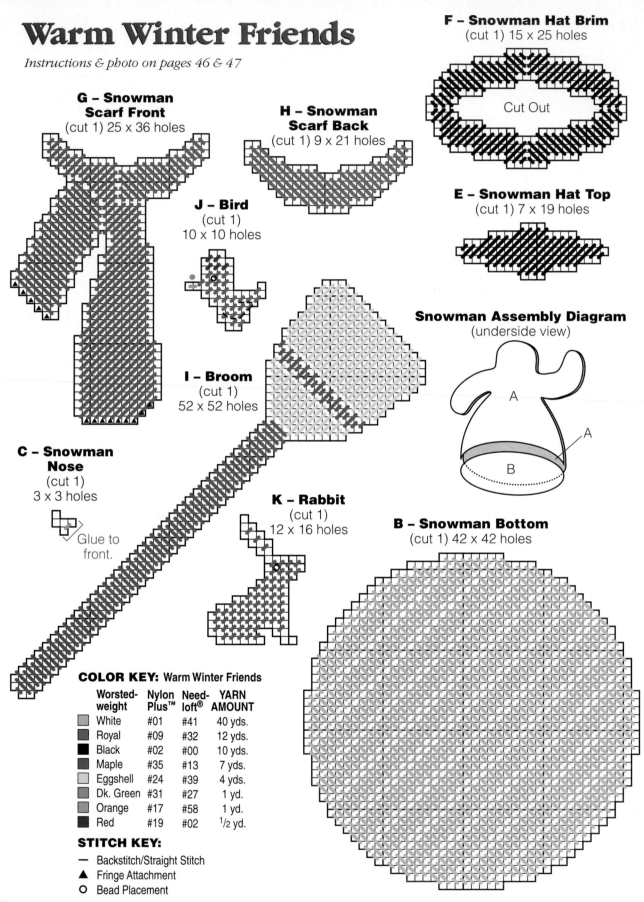

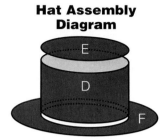
Hat Assembly Diagram

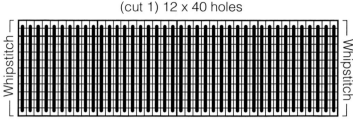

D – Snowman Hat
(cut 1) 12 x 40 holes

Whipstitch   Whipstitch

Christmas Wall Hanging
Instructions & photo on page 44 & 45

COLOR KEY: Christmas Wall Hanging

#3 pearl cotton or floss			AMOUNT
■ Black			2 yds.

Worsted-weight	Nylon Plus™	Need-loft®	YARN AMOUNT
Sail Blue	#04	#35	70 yds.
Eggshell	#24	#39	40 yds.
Forest	#32	#29	40 yds.
Crimson	#53	#42	16 yds.
Dk. Red	#20	#01	14 yds.
Camel	#34	#43	4 yds.
Maple	#35	#13	4 yds.
Tangerine	#15	#11	4 yds.
Black	#02	#00	2 yds.
Dk. Green	#31	#27	1 yd.

STITCH KEY:
- □ Letter Placement
- ● Bead Attachment
- ○ Button Attachment

B – Tree
(cut 2)
39 x 50 holes

D – Broom
(cut 1)
17 x 44 holes

E – Letter Block
(cut 14) 10 x 10 holes

Base Front Stitch Pattern Guide

Continue established pattern up and across entire piece.

Letter Stitch Pattern Guide

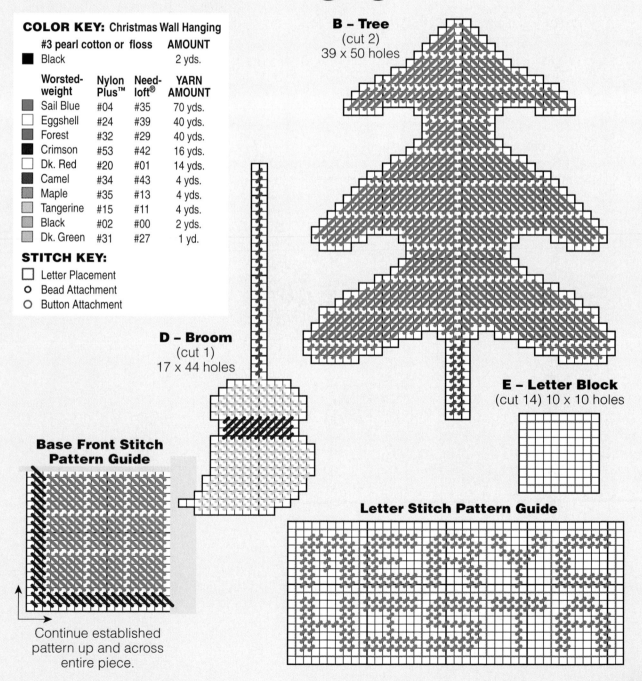

FROSTY FRIENDS

49

We
Believe

Yuletide Traditions

Bells & Bows

SIZE: 7⅜" across x 18½" long, not including bow.

SKILL LEVEL: Average

MATERIALS: Two 12" x 18" or larger sheets of 7-count plastic canvas; Three gold 35-mm jingle bells; 1 yd. gold ½" metallic ribbon; 3½ yds. seasonal 3" ribbon; Craft glue or glue gun; Heavy metallic braid or metallic cord (for amount see Color Key); Worsted-weight or plastic canvas yarn (for amounts see Color Key).

CUTTING INSTRUCTIONS:

A: For front panel, cut one 36 x 120 holes; cut one short end according to graph.

B: For back panel, cut one 48 x 101 holes (no graph).

STITCHING INSTRUCTIONS:

1: Using red and Continental Stitch, work A; Overcast unfinished edges. Leaving uncoded areas unworked and using dk. green and stitches indicated, work B according to Back Panel Stitch Pattern Guide; Overcast edges at stitched areas.

2: Using gold and Backstitch, embroider edge detail on A and B pieces as indicated on graph and stitch pattern guide.

3: With gold, center and sew one bell 5¾" from bottom edge of A, one bell 4⅛" from first bell and remaining bell 3¾" from second bell. Matching straight edges at top, glue unworked area of back panel to center wrong side of front panel (see photo).

NOTE: Cut ½" ribbon into three 12" lengths.

4: Tie each ½" ribbon into a bow; glue above each jingle bell as shown. Tie 2¾" ribbon into a multi-loop bow; glue to top as shown in photo. Hang as desired.❄

– Designed by Betty Radla

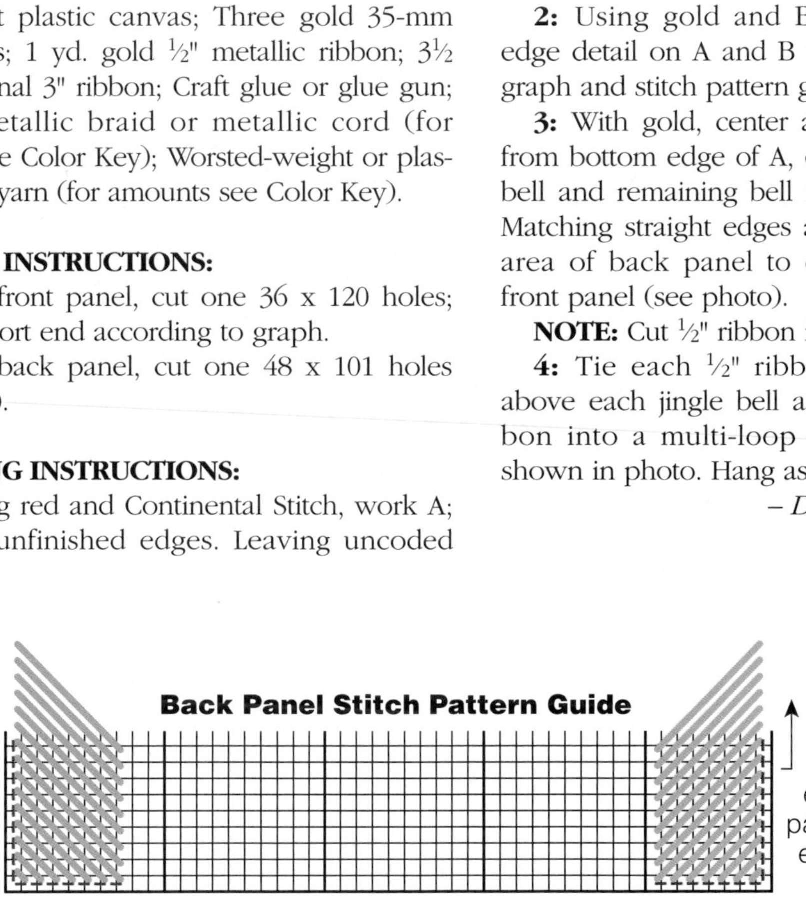
Back Panel Stitch Pattern Guide
Continue established pattern across entire piece.

A – Front Panel (cut 1) 36 x 120 holes

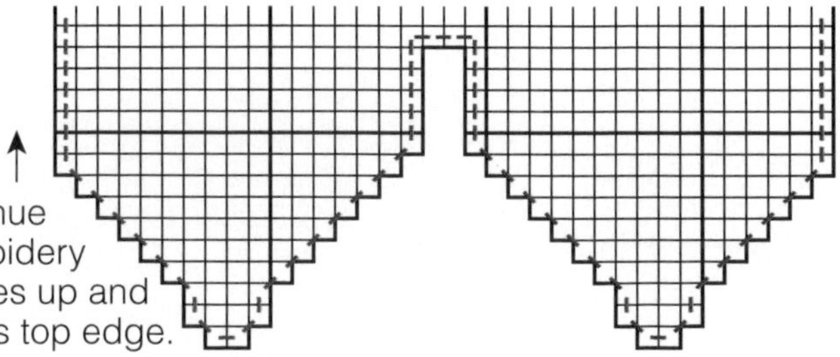
Opposite end is straight across 120 holes from bottom.
Continue embroidery stitches up and across top edge.

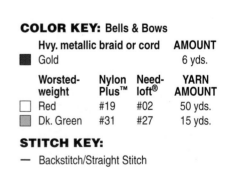

COLOR KEY: Bells & Bows

	Hvy. metallic braid or cord			AMOUNT
■	Gold			6 yds.
	Worsted-weight	**Nylon Plus™**	**Need-loft®**	**YARN AMOUNT**
□	Red	#19	#02	50 yds.
▒	Dk. Green	#31	#27	15 yds.

STITCH KEY:

— Backstitch/Straight Stitch

Hear sleigh bells jingle each time you open the door with this glittery bell pull.

Poinsettias 'round the Room

SIZE: Wreath is about 22" across, not including streamers; Each Candle Holder is about 13" across; Box is 5¼" x 5⅝" x 1¾" tall, not including poinsettia motif; Each Ornament is about 3¾" across.

SKILL LEVEL: Challenging

MATERIALS: 13 sheets of green, 2½ sheets of red, one sheet of white and one sheet of clear stiff 7-count plastic canvas; Two sheets of red, one sheet of green and one sheet of white 10-count plastic canvas; Seven 4¼" plastic canvas radial circles; Two red 15-mm round acrylic stones; 11 gold 15-mm jingle bells; 81 gold 6-mm beads; Four green 1½" pom-poms; 2¼ yds. red 2¼" velveteen ribbon; 12" Styrofoam® extruded floral ring; Two gold 1"-across taper candle cups; ¾ yd. gold fine metallic braid or metallic thread; 8 yds. red and 2 yds. white six-strand embroidery floss; Craft glue or glue gun; Metallic cord (for amount see Color Key on page 61); Worsted-weight or plastic canvas yarn (for amounts see Color Key).

CUTTING INSTRUCTIONS:

NOTE: Graphs & diagrams on pages 59-61.

A: For large poinsettia bases, use 4¼" canvas circles (no graph).

B: For large poinsettia looped bracts, cut eight from red 7-count and forty-eight from green 7-count according to graph.

C: For large poinsettia flat bracts, cut thirteen from red 7-count and eighty from green 7-count according to graph.

D: For small poinsettia bases, cut nine from red 10-count and two from white 10-count according to graph.

E: For small poinsettia looped bracts, cut fifty-four from red 10-count and twelve from white 10-count according to graph.

F: For small poinsettia flat bracts, cut one hundred eight from red 10-count, twenty from green 10-count and sixteen from white 10-count according to graphs.

G: For Box lid and lining, cut one from white 7-count for lid and one from clear stiff 7-count for lining 34 x 37 holes.

H: For Box long sides and linings, cut two from white 7-count for sides and two from clear stiff 7-count for lining 10 x 35 holes.

I: For Box short sides and linings, cut two from white 7-count for sides and two from clear stiff 7-count for lining 10 x 32 holes.

Continued on page 59

NOTE: Melting wax may damage finished items. Use battery powered candles or use for display only.

Season's Greetings Cap

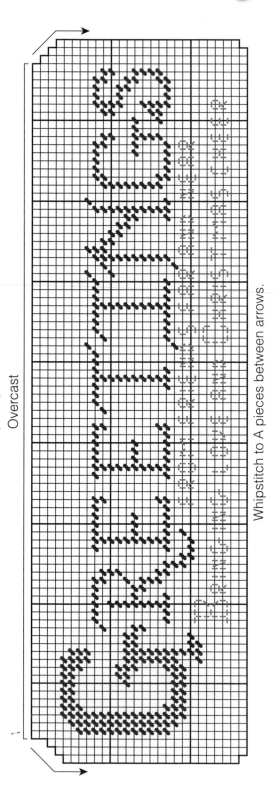

B – Trim (cut 1) 27 x 90 holes
Overcast

Whipstitch to A pieces between arrows.

SIZE: 12¼" x 17½", not including pom-pom.
SKILL LEVEL: Average
MATERIALS: Two 12" x 18" or larger sheets of 7-count plastic canvas; ½ sheet of 7-count plastic canvas; Craft glue or glue gun; Six-strand embroidery floss (for amount see Color Key); Metallic cord (for amount see Color Key); Worsted-weight or plastic canvas yarn (for amounts see Color Key).

CUTTING INSTRUCTIONS:

NOTE: Use one large sheet for each A.

A: For cap front and backing, cut two (one for front and one for backing) according to graph on page 58.

B: For trim, cut one according to graph.

STITCHING INSTRUCTIONS:

NOTE: Backing A is not worked.

1: Using colors and stitches indicated and leaving uncoded areas of A unworked, work front A and B according to graphs; fill in un-coded areas of B using white and Continental Stitch. With white/silver, Overcast top edge of B as indicated on graph.

2: Using six strands floss and Backstitch, embroider letters on B as indicated.

3: Holding backing A to wrong side of front A and B to unworked area on right side of A at matching edges (**NOTE:** B piece is slightly longer than A.), with white/silver, Whipstitch together through all thicknesses as indicated,

COLOR KEY: Seasons Greetings Cap

Embroidery floss			AMOUNT
▉ Green			8 yds.

Metallic cord			AMOUNT
☐ White/Silver			6 yds.

Worsted-weight	Nylon Plus™	Need-loft®	YARN AMOUNT
■ Dk. Red	#20	#01	60 yds.
☐ White	#01	#41	45 yds.
■ Dk. Green	#31	#27	10 yds.

STITCH KEY:
— Backstitch/Straight Stitch

easing B to fit as you work; with dk. red, Whipstitch unfinished edges of A pieces together.

NOTE: Cut one 20-yd. and one 6" length of white.

4: For pom-pom, loosely wrap 20-yd. strand around two fingers; carefully slide loops off fingers. Thread 6" strand through center of loops; tie into a knot to secure. Clip loops; trim pom-pom to 3½". Glue pom-pom to end of cap as shown in photo.❄

– Designed by Trina Taylor Burch

Seasons Greetings Cap

Instructions & photo on pages 56 & 57

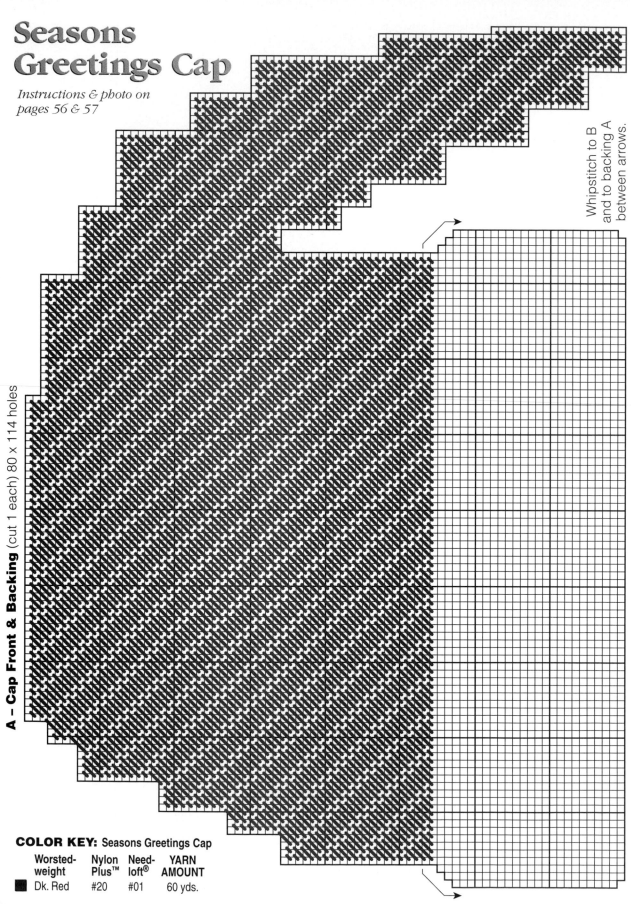

Whipstitch to B and to backing A between arrows.

A – Cap Front & Backing (cut 1 each) 80 x 114 holes

COLOR KEY: Seasons Greetings Cap

	Worsted-weight	Nylon Plus™	Need-loft®	YARN AMOUNT
■	Dk. Red	#20	#01	60 yds.

Poinsettias 'round the Room

Continued from page 54

J: For Box bottom and lining, cut one from white 7-count for bottom and one from clear stiff 7-count for lining 32 x 35 holes (no graph).

STITCHING INSTRUCTIONS:

NOTES: A-F and J pieces are unworked.

Before assembling each flower, soften looped bracts (B and E pieces) with a blow-dry hair dryer set on warm; bend at fold line as indicated on graphs. Dip in cool water to set.

1: For large red poinsettia, matching yarn and canvas color, Whipstitch one A, red B, red C and eight green C pieces together according to Large Red Poinsettia Assembly Diagram on page 61; sew or glue seven bells to flower center as shown in photo. Set poinsettia aside.

2: For each large green poinsettia (make 6), with green yarn, Whipstitch one A, eight B and twelve green C pieces together according to Large Green Poinsettia Assembly Diagram on page 60. Set poinsettias aside.

3: For each small red poinsettia (make 9), with six strands red floss, Whipstitch one red D, six red E, two green E and twelve red F pieces together according to Small Poinsettia Assembly Diagram on page 61. Glue nine gold beads inside center of each flower as shown in photo. Set poinsettias aside.

NOTE: Cut ribbon into three 27" lengths.

4: For Wreath, glue one end of each ribbon to back of foam ring. With red yarn, tie large red poinsettia to front of ring over ribbon attachment; glue to secure. Tie and glue four large green poinsettias around ring as shown; glue one pom-pom, then one small red poinsettia inside center of each large green poinsettia as shown. Glue one small red poinsettia and remaining bells to center streamer; trim streamer ends as shown.

5: For each Candle Holder (make 2), glue one taper cup to center of one large green poinsettia; weave green yarn through base of each center flat bract and pull yarn to raise center bracts, then tie yarn ends together to secure. Glue one small red poinsettia to green poinsettia as shown.

6: For Box, holding one lining piece behind each matching white piece, using gold metallic cord and Slanted Gobelin Stitch, work G-I pieces through both thicknesses as one according to graphs.

7: Arranging pieces to continue stripe pattern, with matching colors, Whipstitch G-J pieces together as indicated and according to Box Assembly Diagram on page 61. Glue one small red poinsettia and remaining loose green F pieces to corner of lid as shown.

8: For red Ornament, tie a 9" length of gold metallic braid or thread to remaining small red poinsettia for hanger as shown.

9: For white Ornaments, using white pieces in place of red and green D-F pieces, make two small poinsettias according to Steps 1 and 2 of Small Poinsettia Assembly Diagram on page 61; glue one red stone to center of each poinsettia as shown. Tie a 9" length of gold metallic braid or thread to each poinsettia for hanger as shown.✻

– Designed by Diane T. Ray

D – Small Poinsettia Base
(cut 9 from red & 2 from white 10-count)
13 x 13 holes

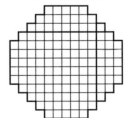

C – Large Poinsettia Flat Bract
(cut 13 from red & 80 from green 7-count)
13 x 28 holes

Poinsettias 'round the Room

Instructions & photo on pages 54 & 55

E – Small Poinsettia Looped Bract
(cut 54 from red & 12 from white 10-count)
7 x 26 holes

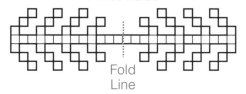

Fold
Line

F – Small Poinsettia Flat Bract
(cut 108 from red, 20 from green & 16
from white 10-count)
7 x 14 holes

G – Box Lid & Lining
(cut 1 from white & 1 from clear) 34 x 37 holes

Whipstitch to one short side to continue stripe pattern.

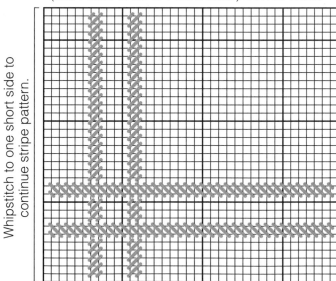

B – Large Poinsettia Looped Bract
(cut 8 from red and 48 from green 7-count)
13 x 53 holes

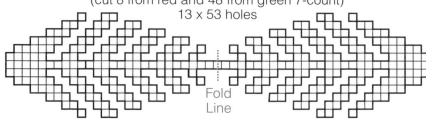

Fold
Line

Large Green Poinsettia Assembly Diagram
(Pieces are shown in different colors for clarity.)

Step 1:
Whipstitch flat ends of 8 green C pieces to first bar inside outer edge of A.

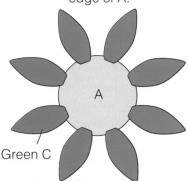

Green C

Step 2:
Holding ends of each shaped B together, Whipstitch to A near center.

Green B

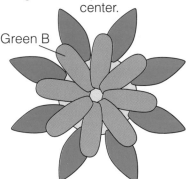

Step 3:
Whipstitch flat ends of four C pieces to center.

Green C

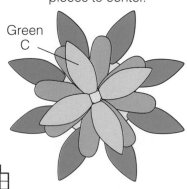

Large Red Poinsettia Assembly Diagram
(Pieces are shown in different colors for clarity.)

Step 1:
Whipstitch flat ends of green C pieces to outside edge; Whipstitch 8 red C pieces to first bar inside outer edge of A.

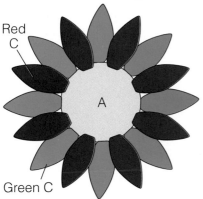

Red C

Green C

A

Step 2:
Holding ends of each shaped B together, Whipstitch to A near center.

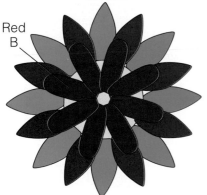

Red B

Step 3:
Whipstitch flat ends of remaining red C pieces to center.

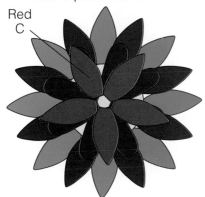

Red C

COLOR KEY: Poinsettias 'round the Room

Metallic cord			AMOUNT
▨ Gold			10 yds.

Worsted-weight	Nylon Plus™	Need-loft®	YARN AMOUNT
☐ Green	#58	#28	8 yds.
☐ White	#01	#41	5 yds.
☐ Red	#19	#02	2 yds.

Box Assembly Diagram

Step 1:
Whipstitch side and bottom edges of H and I pieces together.

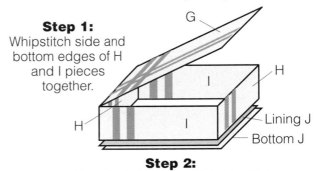

G

H

I

H

I

Lining J

Bottom J

Step 2:
Whipstitch lid to one H; Whipstitch unfinished edges of lid pieces together.

H – Box Long Side & Lining
(cut 2 from white & 2 from clear) 10 x 35 holes

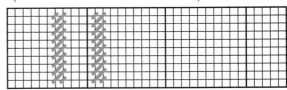

I – Box Short Side & Lining
(cut 2 from white & 2 from clear) 10 x 32 holes

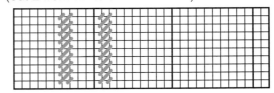

Small Poinsettia Assembly Diagram
(Pieces are shown in different colors for clarity.)

Step 1:
Whipstitch flat ends of 2 green and 8 red F pieces near center of D.

Red F

Green F

D

Step 2:
Holding ends of each shaped E together, Whipstitch to center.

E

Step 3:
Whipstitch remaining red F pieces to center.

Red F

Ornament Coasters

SIZE: Each Coaster is 4½" x 5⅞".

SKILL LEVEL: Easy

MATERIALS: One sheet of 7-count plastic canvas; Heavy metallic braid or metallic cord (for amounts see Color Key on page 67); Worsted-weight or plastic canvas yarn (for amounts see Color Key).

CUTTING INSTRUCTIONS:

A: For Coasters, cut four according to graph on page 67.

STITCHING INSTRUCTIONS:

1: Using colors indicated and Continental Stitch, work one A according to graph. Sub-stituting lavender, lt. yellow and sail blue for fern, and purple, royal and yellow for dk. green, work one remaining A piece in each color combination according to graph (see photo); fill in uncoded areas of A pieces using red and Continental Stitch. With crimson for bow and with matching colors, Overcast edges of A pieces.

2: Using gold braid or cord and Backstitch, embroider bow detail on A pieces as indicated on graph. Using green, purple, royal and yellow braid or cord and Straight Stitch, embroider highlight on one A piece in each corresponding color as indicated.

3: Hang as desired. ❈

– Designed by Rosemarie Walter

Gift Wrapped Doorstop

SIZE: $2\frac{1}{2}$" x $4\frac{1}{8}$" x $7\frac{7}{8}$", not including bow.

SKILL LEVEL: Average

MATERIALS: $1\frac{1}{2}$ sheets of 7-count plastic canvas; Zip-close bag filled with gravel or other weighting material; Craft glue or glue gun; Worsted-weight or plastic canvas yarn (for amounts see Color Key).

CUTTING INSTRUCTIONS:

NOTE: Graphs continued on page 67.

A: For front and back, cut two (one for front and one for back) 26 x 51 holes.

B: For sides, cut two 16 x 51 holes.

C: For top and bottom, cut two (one for top and one for bottom) 16 x 26 holes.

D: For large bow loops, cut four 3 x 31 holes (no graph).

E: For small bow loops, cut four 3 x 24 holes (no graph).

STITCHING INSTRUCTIONS:

1: Using colors and stitches indicated, work A-C pieces according to graphs. Using red and Slanted Gobelin Stitch over narrow width, work D and E pieces.

2: Holding wrong sides together, with forest, Whipstitch A-C pieces together, inserting weight before closing.

3: For each bow loop, holding short ends of one D or E piece wrong sides together, with red, Whipstitch together; Overcast edges. Glue ends of bows together and to intersection of red stitches on front as shown in photo.❋

– Designed by Michele Wilcox

B – Side
(cut 2) 16 x 51 holes

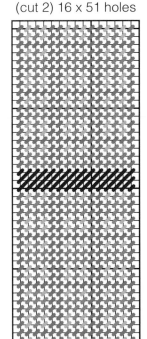

COLOR KEY: Gift Wrapped Doorstop

	Worsted-weight	Nylon Plus™	Need-loft®	YARN AMOUNT
	Forest	#32	#29	35 yds.
	Tangerine	#15	#11	30 yds.
	Red	#19	#02	25 yds.
	White	#01	#41	15 yds.

Country Christmas Kitchen

SIZE: Place Mat is 11⅝" x 15¼"; Each Coaster is 3¾" square; Coaster Holder is 1¾" x 4¼" x 1¾" tall; Each Napkin Ring is 1½" x 1¾".

SKILL LEVEL: Easy

MATERIALS: Two 12" x 18" or larger sheets of 7-count plastic canvas; Two sheets of 7-count plastic canvas; Worsted-weight or plastic canvas yarn (for amounts see Color Key).

CUTTING INSTRUCTIONS:

NOTES: Graphs continued on pages 66 & 67. Use large sheets for A.

A: For Place Mat front and backing, cut two (one for front and one for backing) 76 x 100 holes.

B: For Duck Coaster fronts and backings, cut four (two for fronts and two for backings) 24 x 24 holes.

C: For Check Coaster fronts and backings, cut four (two for fronts and two for backings) 24 x 24 holes.

D: For Coaster Holder sides, cut two 11 x 27 holes.

E: For Coaster Holder ends, cut two 11 x 11 holes.

F: For Coaster Holder bottom, cut one 11 x 27 holes (no graph).

G: For Napkin Rings, cut four 9 x 33 holes.

STITCHING INSTRUCTIONS:

NOTE: Backing A-C and F pieces are not worked.

1: Using colors and stitches indicated, work front A-C, D, E and G pieces according to graphs. Using colors indicated and French Knot, embroider detail on A and B pieces as indicated on graphs.

2: For Place Mat, holding backing A to wrong side of front, with dk. green, Whipstitch together.

3: For each Coaster, holding one backing to wrong side of one front, with dk. green, Whipstitch together. For Coaster Holder, with dk. green, Whipstitch D-F pieces together according to Holder Assembly Diagram on page 67; Overcast unfinished edges.

4: For each Napkin Ring, with dk. green, Whipstitch ends of one F piece together as indicated; Overcast unfinished edges.✳

– Designed by Cherie Marie Leck

*Remember
Christmases past with
traditional holiday motifs.*

B – Duck Coaster
Front & Backing
(cut 2 each) 24 x 24 holes

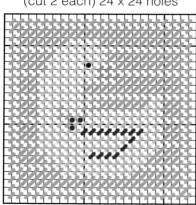

COLOR KEY: Country Christmas Kitchen

Worsted-weight	Nylon Plus™	Need-loft®	YARN AMOUNT
Dk. Red	#20	#01	75 yds.
Dk. Green	#31	#27	63 yds.
White	#01	#41	45 yds.
Pewter	–	#66	4 yds.
Red	#19	#02	2 yds.
Straw	#41	#19	2 yds.
Black	#02	#00	1 yd.

STITCH KEY:
● French Knot

C – Check Coaster
Front & Backing
(cut 2 each) 24 x 24 holes

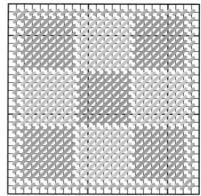

Country Christmas Kitchen Instructions & photos on pages 64 & 65

A – Place Mat Front & Backing (cut 1 each) 76 x 100 holes

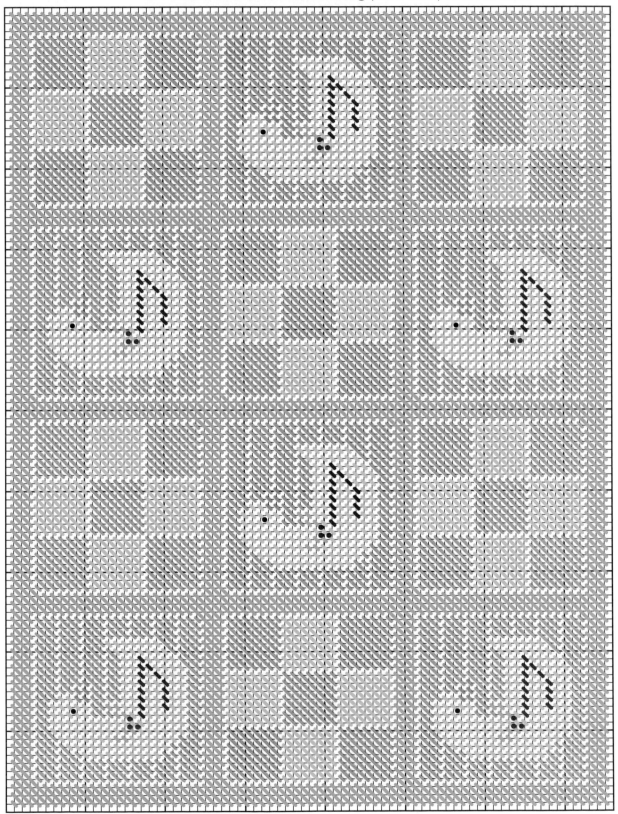

COLOR KEY: Country Christmas Kitchen

	Worsted-weight	Nylon Plus™	Need-loft®	YARN AMOUNT
	Dk. Red	#20	#01	75 yds.
	Dk. Green	#31	#27	63 yds.
	White	#01	#41	45 yds.
	Pewter	–	#66	4 yds.
	Red	#19	#02	2 yds.
	Straw	#41	#19	2 yds.
	Black	#02	#00	1 yd.

STITCH KEY:

● French Knot

Holder Assembly Diagram

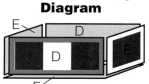

E – Coaster Holder End
(cut 2)
11 x 11 holes

D – Coaster Holder Side
(cut 2) 11 x 27 holes

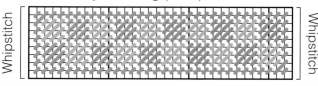

G – Napkin Ring (cut 4) 9 x 33 holes

Whipstitch   Whipstitch

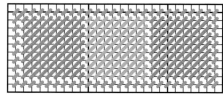

Gift Wrapped Doorstop

Instructions & photo on page 63

COLOR KEY: Gift Wrapped Doorstop

	Worsted-weight	Nylon Plus™	Need-loft®	YARN AMOUNT
	Forest	#32	#29	35 yds.
	Tangerine	#15	#11	30 yds.
	Red	#19	#02	25 yds.
	White	#01	#41	15 yds.

C – Top & Bottom
(cut 1 each) 16 x 26 holes

A – Front & Back
(cut 1 each) 26 x 51 holes

Ornament Coasters

Instructions & photo on page 62

COLOR KEY: Ornament Coasters

	Heavy metallic braid	AMOUNT
	Gold	5 yds.
	Green	½ yd.
	Purple	½ yd.
	Royal	½ yd.
	Yellow	½ yd.
	Highlight color	

	Worsted-weight	Nylon Plus™	Need-loft®	YARN AMOUNT
	Red	#19	#02	18 yds.
	Crimson	#53	#42	12 yds.
	Fern	#57	#23	4 yds.
	Lavender	#22	#45	4 yds.
	Lt. Yellow	#42	#21	4 yds.
	Sail Blue	#04	#35	4 yds.
	Dk. Green	#31	#27	2½ yds.
	Purple	#21	#46	2½ yds.
	Royal	#09	#32	2½ yds.
	Yellow	#26	#57	2½ yds.
	White	#01	#41	2 yds.

STITCH KEY:

— Backstitch/Straight Stitch

A – Coaster
(cut 4)
29 x 38 holes

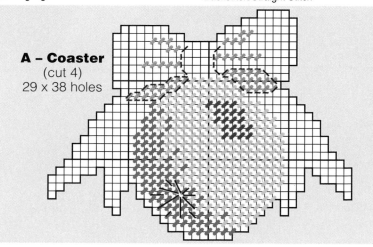

Country Decor

SIZE: Each is 3⅞" x 10¾", not including tassel.

SKILL LEVEL: Easy

MATERIALS FOR ONE: ⅓ sheet each of clear and white 7-count plastic canvas; One 3½" x 4" piece of Christmas motif fabric; One 3½" x 4" piece of posterboard; Fusible web-bing; One desired color 15-mm jingle bell; Worsted-weight or plastic canvas yarn (for amounts see individual Color Keys).

CUTTING INSTRUCTIONS:

A: For front and backing, cut two (one from clear for front and one from white for backing)

according to graph of choice.

STITCHING INSTRUCTIONS:

NOTE: Backing A is not worked.

1: Using colors and stitches indicated, work front A according to graph of choice; with red, Overcast edges of large cutout.

2: For "We Believe," using white and embroidery stitches indicated, embroider letters on front A as indicated on graph.

NOTE: Center fabric motif over posterboard; attach with fusible webbing according to manufacturer's instructions.

3: Glue right side of fabric motif over large cutout on wrong side of A (see photo). Holding backing A to wrong side of front, with red, Whipstitch outside and small cutout edges together. If desired, with matching color, tack front and back pieces together as indicated.

NOTE: Cut three 12" and one 6" length of red.

4: For tassel, thread one end of one 12" strand through ✦ hole, and thread one end of each remaining 12" strand through ▲ hole as indicated; pull ends to even. Wrap 6" strand around 12" strands ¾" from bottom edge of Hanger, securing ends under wraps as you work. Tie bell onto one strand just below wraps (see photo). Trim ends of tassel to even.❄

– Designed by Anne DiGeorge

COLOR KEY: Sugar 'N Spice

	Worsted-weight	Nylon Plus™	Need-loft®	YARN AMOUNT
■	White	#01	#41	16 yds.
□	Red	#19	#02	6 yds.
▨	Dk. Green	#31	#27	2 yds.

STITCH KEY:
- □ Cut out for front only.

COLOR KEY: We Believe

	Worsted-weight	Nylon Plus™	Need-loft®	YARN AMOUNT
▨	Dk. Green	#31	#27	15 yds.
▨	Red	#19	#02	8 yds.
■	White	#01	#41	2 yds.

STITCH KEY:
- — Backstitch/Straight Stitch
- □ Cut out for front only.

A – "We Believe" Front & Backing
(cut 1 from each color)
25 x 70 holes

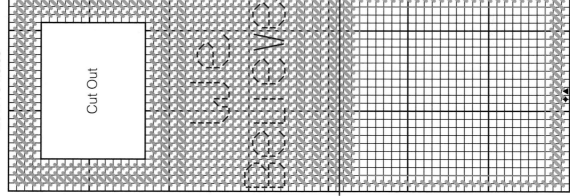

Tack

Cut Out

A – "Sugar 'N Spice" Front & Backing
(cut 1 from each color)
25 x 70 holes

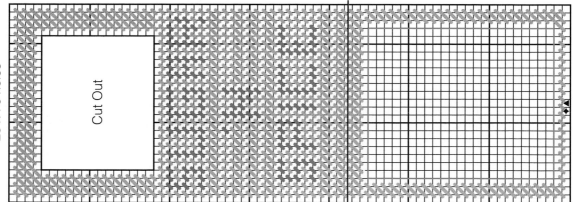

Tack

Cut Out

Gifts from Santa

Light up someone's holiday with these adorable earrings.

Candy Cane Earrings
Instructions on page 77

Merry Lights Earrings

SIZE: Each Earring is ¾" x 1¼".
SKILL LEVEL: Easy
MATERIALS FOR ONE PAIR: Scraps of 14-count plastic canvas; Two gold fishhook ear wires; Medium metallic braid or metallic thread (for amount see Color Key); #5 pearl cotton or six-strand embroidery floss (for amounts see Color Key).

CUTTING INSTRUCTIONS:
A: For Bulbs, cut two according to graph.

STITCHING INSTRUCTIONS:
1: Using colors indicated and Continental Stitch, work according to graph. With matching colors, Overcast edges.

2: Using white and Straight Stitch, embroider highlights as indicated on graph.

3: Attach one ear wire through center top hole on each Bulb (see photo).❋
– *Designed by Cherie Marie Leck*

A – Bulb
(cut 2)
9 x 16 holes

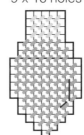

COLOR KEY: Merry Lights Earrings

Med. metallic braid or thread	AMOUNT
▢ Gold	1 yd.

#5 pearl cotton or floss	AMOUNT
▨ Color of choice	3 yds.
■ White	½ yd.

STITCH KEY:
— Backstitch/Straight Stitch

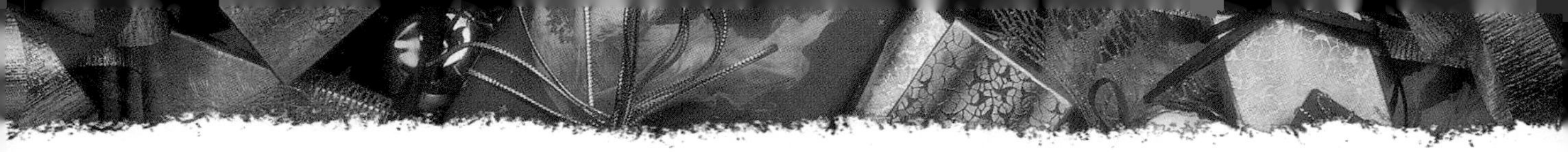

"Ho Ho Ho" Pin

SIZE: 2⅜" x 2⅞".

SKILL LEVEL: Average

MATERIALS: One 3" plastic canvas radial circle; ¼ sheet of 10-count plastic canvas; One ½" pinback; Craft glue or glue gun; $\frac{1}{16}$" metallic ribbon (for amounts see Color Key); Raffia straw (for amount see Color Key); Worsted-weight or plastic canvas yarn (for amounts see Color Key).

CUTTING INSTRUCTIONS:

A: For words, cut three according to graph.

B: For holly leaves, cut four according to graph.

C: For wreath, cut one from 3" circle according to graph.

STITCHING INSTRUCTIONS:

1: Using colors and stitches indicated, work A (substitute gold for Christmas on one A piece) and B pieces according to graphs. With matching colors, Overcast edges.

2: Wrap wreath with raffia until completely covered, securing ends of raffia under wraps as you work. Using red and French Knot, embroider holly berries on B pieces as indicated on graph and on C, if desired.

3: Glue leaves and words to front and pinback to back of wreath as shown in photo.❄

– Designed by Kathleen Kennebeck

C – Wreath
(cut 1 from 3" circle)
Cut away gray areas.

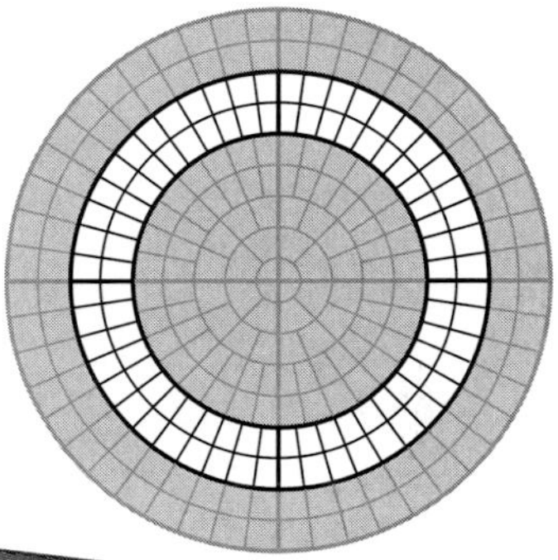

B – Holly Leaf
(cut 4)
7 x 11 holes

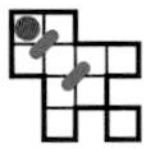

A – "Ho"
(cut 3) 7 x 11 holes

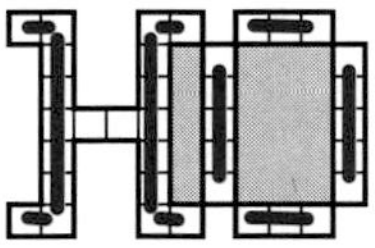

Cut out gray areas carefully.

COLOR KEY: "Ho Ho Ho" Pin

	Kreinik $\frac{1}{16}$" metallic ribbon			AMOUNT
■	#238 Christmas			4 yds.
□	#002HL Gold			2 yds.
	Raffia straw			**AMOUNT**
□	Green			6 yds.
	Worsted-weight	**Nylon Plus™**	**Need-loft®**	**YARN AMOUNT**
■	Green	#58	#28	1 yd.
■	Red	#19	#02	½ yd.

STITCH KEY:

- ● French Knot

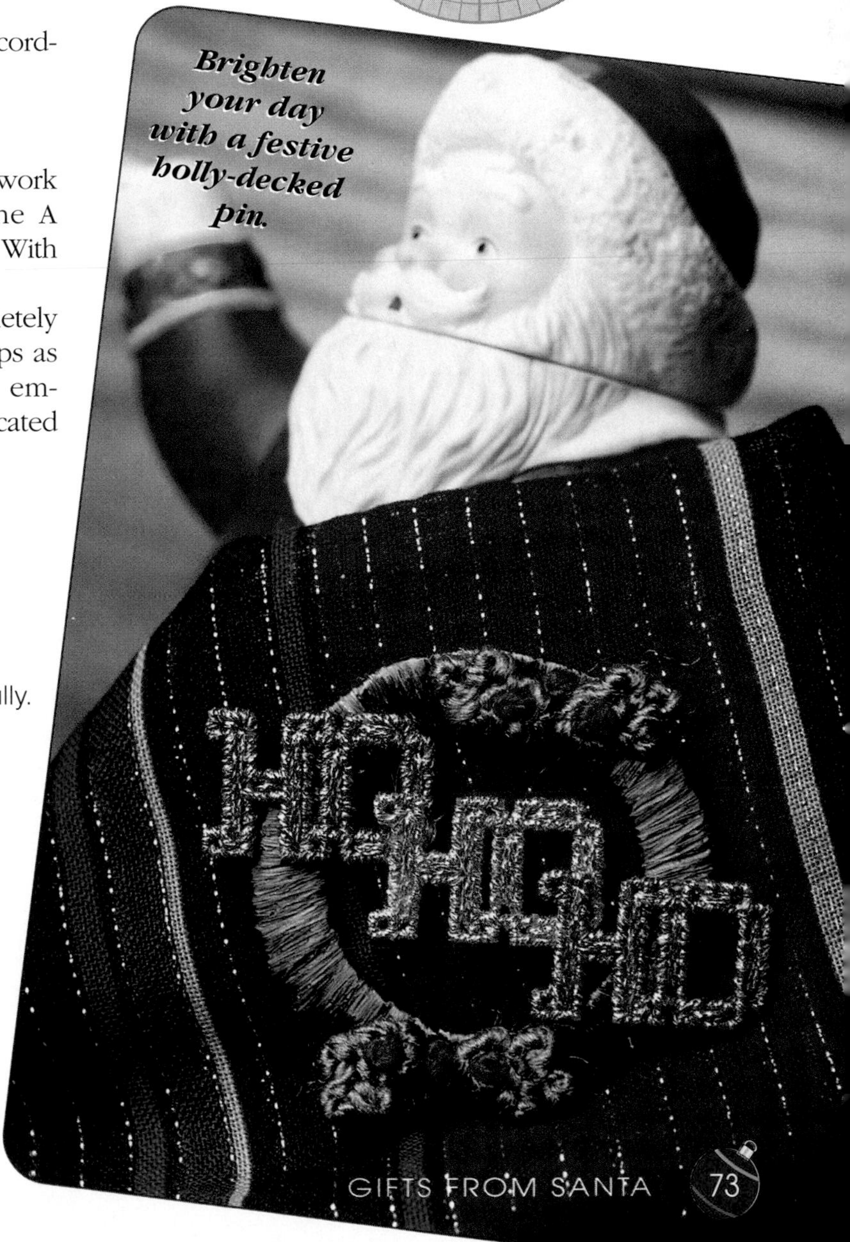

Brighten your day with a festive holly-decked pin.

Precious Pet

SIZE: 4½" x 7½" x 11" tall, including tail.

SKILL LEVEL: Average

MATERIALS: Two sheets of 7-count plastic canvas; Polyester fiberfill; Worsted-weight or plastic canvas yarn (for amounts see Color Key).

CUTTING INSTRUCTIONS:

NOTE: Graphs continued on pages 76 & 77.

A: For head front, cut one according to graph.

B: For head back, cut one according to graph.

C: For body front, cut one according to graph.

D: For body back, cut one according to graph.

E: For top sides #1 and #2, cut one each according to graphs.

F: For bottom sides, cut two 13 x 24 holes.

G: For bottom, cut one 13 x 32 holes (no graph).

H: For tail, cut one according to graph.

STITCHING INSTRUCTIONS:

NOTE: Use Continental Stitch throughout.

1: Using colors indicated, work A-F and H pieces according to graphs; fill in uncoded areas of A-F (leave indicated area of B unworked) pieces using eggshell. Using beige, work G. With dk. brown, Overcast edges of H as indicated on graph.

2: Using colors and embroidery stitches indicated, embroider facial detail on A and foot detail on C as indicated on graphs.

3: Whipstitch and assemble pieces and fiberfill as indicated and according to Cat Assembly Diagram on page 77. ✳

– Designed by Diane T. Ray

COLOR KEY: Precious Pet

	Worsted-weight	Nylon Plus™	Need-loft®	YARN AMOUNT
	Eggshell	#24	#39	48 yds.
	Beige	#43	#40	38 yds.
	Dk. Brown	#36	#15	23 yds.
	Camel	#34	#43	6 yds.
	Black	#02	#00	2 yds.
	Turquoise	#03	#54	½ yd.
	White	#01	#41	¼ yd.

STITCH KEY:
- — Backstitch/Straight Stitch
- • French Knot
- ☐ Unworked Area/Body & Head Attachment

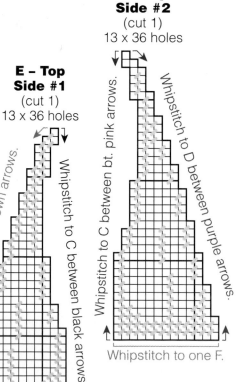

E – Top Side #2
(cut 1)
13 x 36 holes

Whipstitch to D between pink arrows.

Whipstitch to C between bt. pink arrows.

Whipstitch to D between purple arrows.

Whipstitch to one F.

E – Top Side #1
(cut 1)
13 x 36 holes

Whipstitch to D between lt. brown arrows.

Whipstitch to C between black arrows.

Whipstitch to one F.

F – Bottom Side
(cut 2) 13 x 24 holes

Whipstitch to one E.

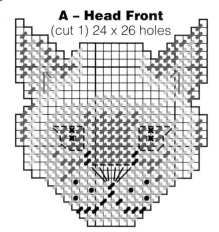

A – Head Front
(cut 1) 24 x 26 holes

Enjoy the company of an elegant and posable Siamese kitty with an eye full of mischief.

Precious Pet

Instructions & photo on pages 74 & 75

COLOR KEY: Precious Pet

Worsted-weight	Nylon Plus™	Need-loft®	YARN AMOUNT
☐ Eggshell	#24	#39	48 yds.
☐ Beige	#43	#40	38 yds.
☐ Dk. Brown	#36	#15	23 yds.
☐ Camel	#34	#43	6 yds.
■ Black	#02	#00	2 yds.
☐ Turquoise	#03	#54	1/2 yd.
☐ White	#01	#41	1/4 yd.

STITCH KEY:

— Backstitch/Straight Stitch

• French Knot

☐ Unworked Area/Body & Head Attachment

D – Body Back (cut 1) 38 x 59 holes

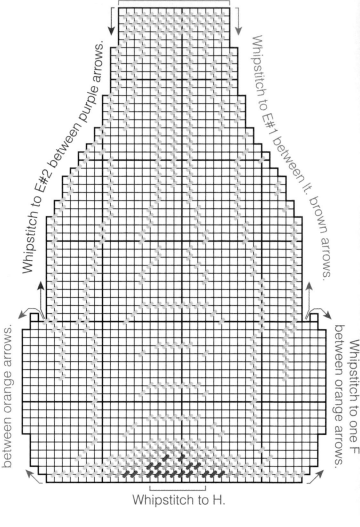

Whipstitch to B.

Whipstitch to E#2 between purple arrows.

Whipstitch to E#1 between lt. brown arrows.

Whipstitch to one F between orange arrows.

Whipstitch to one F between orange arrows.

Whipstitch to H.

C – Body Front
(cut 1) 38 x 57 holes

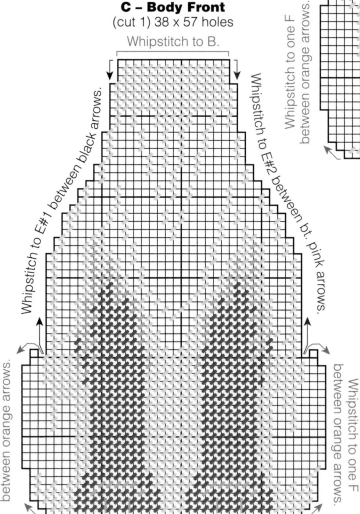

Whipstitch to B.

Whipstitch to E#1 between black arrows.

Whipstitch to E#2 between bt. pink arrows.

Whipstitch to one F between orange arrows.

Whipstitch to one F between orange arrows.

B – Head Back
(cut 1) 24 x 26 holes

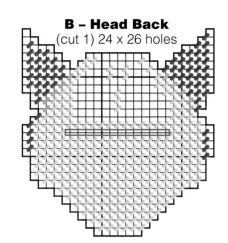

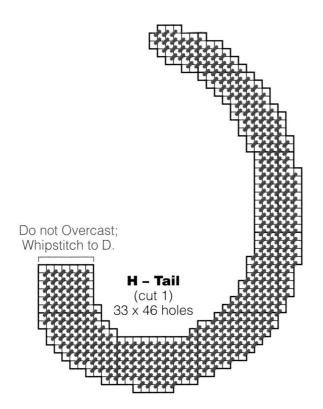

Do not Overcast;
Whipstitch to D.

H – Tail
(cut 1)
33 x 46 holes

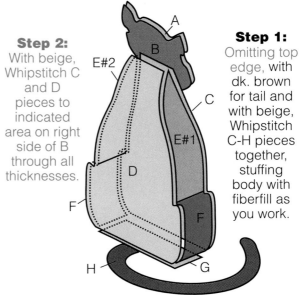

Cat Assembly Diagram
(back view; pieces are shown in
different colors for contrast.)

Step 3:
With dk. brown for ears (see photo) and
with beige, Whipstitch A and B pieces
wrong sides together.

Step 2:
With beige,
Whipstitch C
and D
pieces to
indicated
area on right
side of B
through all
thicknesses.

Step 1:
Omitting top
edge, with
dk. brown
for tail and
with beige,
Whipstitch
C-H pieces
together,
stuffing
body with
fiberfill as
you work.

A

B

E#2

E#1

C

D

F

F

H

G

Candy Cane Earrings

Photo on page 72

SIZE: Each Earring is ¾" x 1½".
SKILL LEVEL: Average
MATERIALS: Scraps of 10-count plastic canvas; Two ear wires; Beading or #9 quilting needle and white quilting thread; Four white and 26 red seed beads; Blending filament (for amount see Color Key); Six-strand embroidery floss (for amount see Color Key); ¹⁄₁₆" ribbon floss (for amount see Color Key).

CUTTING INSTRUCTIONS:

A: For candy canes, cut two according to graph.

STITCHING INSTRUCTIONS:

1: Using white and Continental Stitch, work A pieces on opposite sides of canvas according to graph; Overcast edges.
2: Holding four strands floss together with four strands blending filament, wrap pieces as

indicated on graph, securing ends under stitches on wrong side.
3: With one strand floss, sew red beads to pieces as indicated, working over wrap stitches on wrong side to secure wraps.
4: For each earring, tie a doubled strand of thread in a knot at top of piece. Beginning with red and alternating colors, thread three beads on strand. Thread one white bead on wire, and push bead up over wire loop. Take thread over wire on loop and go back down through beads; pull thread so beads are against canvas and wire. Secure thread with knot on wrong side.✷
— *Designed by Kathleen Kennebeck*

COLOR KEY: Candy Cane

	Blending filament	AMOUNT
☐	Red	2 yds.
	Embroidery floss	**AMOUNT**
■	Red	1 yd.
	¹⁄₁₆" ribbon floss:	**AMOUNT**
☐	White	2 yds.

STITCH KEY:
− Backstitch/Straight Stitch
o Bead Attachment

A – Candy Cane
(cut 2)
7 x 15 holes

Bougainvillea Frame

SIZE: 8½" x 10½" with a 5½" x 7½" photo window.

SKILL LEVEL: Average

MATERIALS: Two sheets of regular flexibility and ½ sheet of stiff 7-count plastic canvas; 1" x 7¾" piece of white cardboard; 8" x 10" piece of acrylic glass; Ten 1½" pieces of green cloth-covered 24-gauge floral wire; 30 white 6-mm baby's breath beads; 30 yellow double-headed flower stamens; Craft glue or glue gun; Worsted-weight or plastic canvas yarn (for amounts see Color Key).

CUTTING INSTRUCTIONS:

NOTE: Use stiff for C and regular flexibility canvas for remaining pieces.

A: For front, cut one according to graph.

B: For back, cut one 55 x 69 holes (no graph).

C: For support pieces, cut two 19 x 53 holes.

D: For flower petals, cut thirty according to graph.

Continued on page 92

C – Support Piece
(cut 2) 9 x 53 holes
Whipstitch to B.

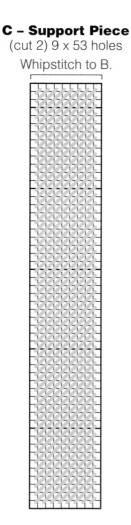

A – Front (cut 1) 55 x 69 holes
Whipstitch between arrows.

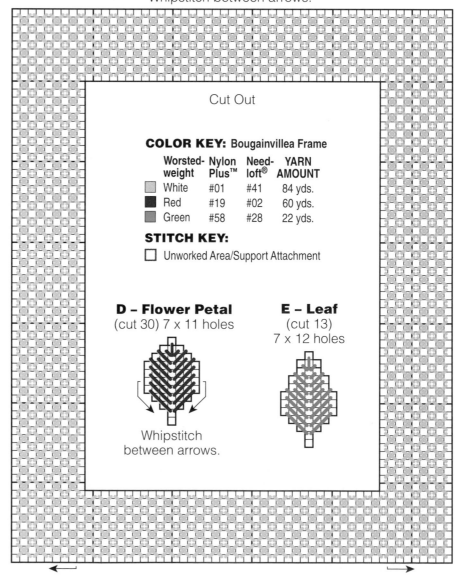

Cut Out

COLOR KEY: Bougainvillea Frame

	Worsted-weight	Nylon Plus™	Need-loft®	YARN AMOUNT
White		#01	#41	84 yds.
Red		#19	#02	60 yds.
Green		#58	#28	22 yds.

STITCH KEY:

☐ Unworked Area/Support Attachment

D – Flower Petal
(cut 30) 7 x 11 holes

Whipstitch between arrows.

E – Leaf
(cut 13)
7 x 12 holes

Surround a treasured photo in an enchanting holiday arrangement of fresh blooming flowers.

Nutcracker Soldier

SIZE: Snugly covers a boutique-style tissue box.

SKILL LEVEL: Average

MATERIALS: Two sheets of 7-count plastic canvas; Craft glue or glue gun; Worsted-weight or plastic canvas yarn; for amounts see Color Key.

CUTTING INSTRUCTIONS:

NOTE: Graphs continued on page 93.

A: For sides, cut four 30 x 36 holes.

B: For top, cut one according to graph.

C: For hat, cut one according to graph.

D: For plume, cut one according to graph.

E: For face, cut one according to graph.

F: For left side hair, cut one according to graph.

G: For right side hair, cut one according to graph.

H: For straps, cut one according to graph.

I: For arms, cut two 7 x 12 holes.

J: For hands, cut two according to graph.

K: For epaulets, cut two according to graph.

L: For feet, cut two according to graph.

STITCHING INSTRUCTIONS:

1: Using colors and stitches indicated, work pieces according to graphs; with matching colors, Overcast edges of C-L pieces and cutout edges of B.

2: Using red and Straight Stitch, embroider mouth on E as indicated on graph.

3: With royal, Whipstitch A and B pieces together, forming Cover; Overcast unfinished bottom edges. Glue C-L pieces to one side of Cover as shown in photo.✷

– Designed by Sandra Miller Maxfield

B – Top
(cut 1) 30 x 30 holes

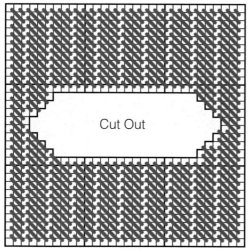

Cut Out

Wrapping Creatively

JUST FOR GRANDMA – There's nothing more beautiful than a grandchild's artwork. Measure and cut freezer paper required for gift. Add kids and crayons and watch their creativity flow.

COLOR KEY: Nutcracker Soldier

	Worsted-weight	Nylon Plus™	Need-loft®	YARN AMOUNT
■	Royal	#09	#32	36 yds.
■	Black	#02	#00	10 yds.
▨	Lt. Pink	#10	#08	6 1/2 yds.
■	Red	#19	#02	6 yds.
□	Yellow	#26	#57	5 yds.
▨	White	#01	#41	4 yds.
■	Pink	#11	#07	1/2 yd.

STITCH KEY:

— Backstitch/Straight Stitch

C – Hat (cut 1) 16 x 30 holes

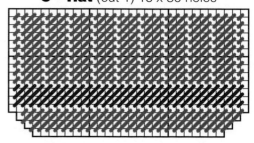

*Stand guard against stuffy
noses during the winter
season with this festive cover.*

Chef Piggy

SIZE: Cookie Jar is about 6¼" across x about 14" tall, including hat, and holds a 42 oz. cardboard oats container; Menu Board is 9½" x about 20" long, including hat; Magnet is 2½" x 5", including hat.

SKILL LEVEL: Challenging

MATERIALS: One 13½" x 22½" sheet and three regular-size sheets of 7-count plastic canvas; ¼ sheet of 10-count plastic canvas; One 6" plastic canvas radial circle; One 2" x 27" strip of yellow gingham fabric; One 18" x 28" piece of white broadcloth fabric; Four black 15-mm and two black 6-mm round cabochons; 12 gold 3-mm beads; Beading or #9 quilting needle and gold thread; Sewing needle or machine and white thread; 42 oz. empty oats container; Polyester fiberfill; One 8¾" x 11½" chalkboard; Pink acrylic paint; Seven round ¾" magnets; Two 1½" magnetic strips; Craft glue or glue gun; #3 pearl cotton or six-strand embroidery floss (for amounts see Color Key on page 84); Metallic cord (for amount see Color Key); Worsted-weight or plastic canvas yarn (for amounts see Color Key).

COOKIE JAR

CUTTING INSTRUCTIONS:

NOTES: Graphs on pages 84 & 85.

Use large sheet for A and C, remainder of large sheet and regular-size sheets for D-N and 10-count canvas for O pieces.

A: For body, cut one 62 x 120 holes (no graph).

B: For bottom, cut away one outer row of holes from circle (no graph).

C: For hatband, cut one 9 x 128 holes (no graph).

D: For bib, cut one according to graph.

E: For arm pieces, cut four according to graph.

F: For leg pieces, cut four according to graph.

G: For snout front, cut one according to graph.

H: For snout side, cut one 4 x 38 holes (no graph).

I: For mouth sides, cut two according to graph.

J: For cheeks, cut two according to graph.

K: For outer ears, cut two according to graph.

L: For inner ears, cut two according to graph.

M: For tail pieces, cut two according to graph.

N: For cookie sheet, cut two 19 x 29 holes (no graph).

O: For cookies, cut six according to graph.

STITCHING INSTRUCTIONS:

NOTES: B piece is not worked.

Use Continental Stitch throughout.

1: Using yarn and pearl cotton or six strands floss in colors indicated, work A (overlap five holes at ends and work through both thicknesses at overlap areas to join), D-F (two of each E and F on opposite side of canvas), G, I-M (one of each I and M on opposite side of canvas) and O pieces according to stitch pattern guide and graphs. Using white for hatband, pink for snout side and silver for cookie sheet, work C, H (overlap five holes at ends of C and two holes at ends of H and work through both thicknesses of each piece at overlap areas to join) and N pieces. With matching colors, Overcast edges of C, D, J and O pieces.

2: Using pearl cotton or six strands floss in colors and embroidery stitches indicated, embroider eyelashes on A as indicated on graph and chocolate chips on O pieces as indicated or as desired. For bib, using #9 quilting or beading needle and gold thread, sew 3-mm beads to D as indicated.

3: With pink, Whipstitch B to bottom edge of A; Overcast edge of body. For each arm and leg, with matching colors, Whipstitch two E or F pieces wrong sides together, stuffing with fiberfill before closing.

4: With pink, Whipstitch G and H pieces together, forming snout, and I pieces wrong sides

Continued on page 84

Let these charming
piggies lend a
helpful hoof in your
baking success.

Chef Piggy

Continued from page 82

together as indicated, forming mouth; Overcast unfinished edges of snout and mouth.

5: For each outer ear, with pink, Whipstitch Y edges of one K piece wrong sides together as indicated; for each inner ear, with lt. pink, Whipstitch Y edges of one L right sides together as indicated. Overcast unfinished edges of ear pieces. For each ear, glue one L and one K wrong sides together.

6: Glue bib, arms, legs, snout, mouth, cheeks, ears and two 15-mm cabochons to center front of body as shown in photo.

NOTE: Cut one 16" circle from one end of broadcloth; cut one 2" x 24" strip of gingham.

7: Fold broadcloth fabric edges under ¼" and machine or hand baste with gathering stitches. Gather fabric to fit inside hatband; machine or hand sew gathers around one edge of hatband. Fold gingham fabric edges under ¼" on each long end and press; fold strip in half lengthwise with wrong sides together and press. Wrap strip around pig as shown and tie into a knot at front; trim ends as desired. Glue each end of strip to bib to secure.

8: For cookie sheet, with silver, Whipstitch N pieces wrong sides together. Glue cookies to cookie sheet and cookie sheet to arms and body front as shown.

9: Place container inside and hat on head of assembly.

Cookie Jar Body Stitch Pattern Guide

Continue established pattern across entire piece.

Continue established pattern across entire piece.

Center of Canvas

COLOR KEY: Chef Piggy

#3 pearl cotton or floss			AMOUNT
Med. Brown			12 yds.
Dk. Brown			5 yds.
Black			4 yds.

Metallic cord			AMOUNT
Silver			26 yds.

Worsted-weight	Nylon Plus™	Need-loft®	YARN AMOUNT
Pink	#11	#07	3½ oz.
White	#01	#41	87 yds.
Black	#02	#00	17 yds.
Lt. Pink	#10	#08	3 yds.
Maple	#35	#13	2 yds.

STITCH KEY:
— Backstitch/Straight Stitch
o Bib Bead Attachment

J – Cookie Jar Cheek
(cut 2) 8 x 8 holes

K – Cookie Jar Outer Ear
(cut 2) 11 x 14 holes

Whipstitch Y edges together.

D – Cookie Jar Bib
(cut 1) 17 x 20 holes

L – Cookie Jar Inner Ear
(cut 2) 9 x 12 holes

Whipstitch Y edges together.

MENU BOARD

CUTTING INSTRUCTIONS:

NOTE: Graphs on page 87.

A: For head front and backing, cut two (one for front and one for backing) according to graph.

B: For hatband front and backing, cut two (one for front and one for backing) 8 x 25 holes (no graph).

C: For snout front, cut one according to graph.

D: For snout side, cut one 5 x 45 holes (no graph).

E: For mouth pieces, cut two according to graph.

F: For cheeks, cut two according to Cookie Jar J graph on page 84.

G: For outer ears, cut two according to Cookie Jar K graph.

H: For inner ears, cut two according to Cookie Jar L graph.

I: For spatula, cut one according to graph.

J: For spoon, cut one according to graph.

K: For hooves, cut four according to graph.

L: For letters and punctuation, cut one each according to graphs.

M: For tail pieces, cut two according to graph.

N: For chalk holder sides and bottom, cut three (two for sides and one for bottom) 4 x 24 holes (no graph).

O: For chalk holder ends, cut two 4 x 4 holes (no graph).

STITCHING INSTRUCTIONS:

NOTES: Backing A and B pieces are not worked.

Use Continental Stitch throughout.

1: Using colors indicated, work one A for front, C, E-K and M (one E, two K and one M piece on opposite side of canvas) pieces according to graphs. Using white for hatband and pink for snout side and chalk holder pieces, work one B for front, D (overlap two holes at ends and work through both thicknesses at overlap area to join), N and O pieces. With pink for letters and punctuation and with matching colors, Overcast edges of F and I-L pieces.

2: Using pearl cotton or six strands black floss and Straight Stitch, embroider eyelashes on front A as indicated on graph.

3: Holding backing A to wrong side of front, with pink, Whipstitch together as indicated; Overcast unfinished edges of front. For hatband, holding backing B to wrong side of front, with white, Whipstitch short edges together;

Continued on page 86

E – Cookie Jar Arm Piece

(cut 4) 18 x 19 holes

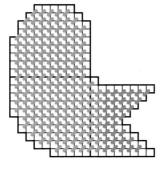

G – Cookie Jar Snout Front

(cut 1) 10 x 12 holes

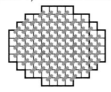

I – Cookie Jar Mouth Side

(cut 2) 4 x 7 holes

Glue to body. Whipstitch

F – Cookie Jar Leg Piece

(cut 4) 14 x 19 holes

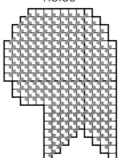

O – Cookie Jar Cookie

(cut 6 from 10-count) 8 x 8 holes

M – Cookie Jar Tail Piece

(cut 2) 6 x 10 holes

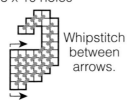

Whipstitch between arrows.

Chef Piggy

Continued from page 85

Overcast unfinished edges of front.

4: Substituting C and D pieces for G and H pieces and E for I, follow Step 4 of Cookie Jar on page 83.

5: Substituting G and H pieces for K and L pieces, follow Step 5 of Cookie Jar.

6: With pink, Whipstitch M pieces wrong sides together, forming tail. Whipstitch N and O pieces together according to Chalk Holder Assembly Diagram; Overcast unfinished edges.

NOTE: Paint wood on chalkboard; let dry.

7: Insert one end of chalkboard into open area of head between front and back (see photo); glue to secure. Glue snout, mouth, cheeks, ears and remaining 15-mm cabochons to head as shown. Glue spatula, spoon, hooves, letters and punctuation, chalk holder and tail to chalkboard as shown. Glue round magnets evenly spaced around wood on back of chalkboard.

NOTE: Cut one 12" circle of broadcloth; cut one 2" x 12" strip of gingham.

8: Substituting 12" circle for 16" circle and 2" x 12" strip for 2" x 24" strip, follow Step 7 of Cookie Jar. Insert head top into hatband as shown and glue to secure.

MAGNET

CUTTING INSTRUCTIONS:

A: For head, cut one according to graph.

B: For hatband front and backing, cut two (one for front and one for backing) 4 x 9 holes (no graph).

C: For snout pieces, cut four according to graph.

D: For mouth sides, cut two 1 x 3 holes (no graph).

E: For cheeks, cut two according to graph.

F: For ears, cut two according to graph.

STITCHING INSTRUCTIONS:

NOTE: Backing B is not worked.

1: Using pink and Continental Stitch, work A, C (hold pieces together and work through all thicknesses as one piece), E and F pieces according to graphs. Using white and Continental Stitch, work one B for front. With pink, Overcast edges of A and E pieces; Whipstitch edges of C together through all thicknesses as one piece.

2: Using pearl cotton or six strands black floss, embroider eyelashes on A and nostrils on B as indicated on graphs.

3: For each ear, Whipstitch Y edges of one F right sides together; Overcast unfinished edges. For hatband, holding backing B to wrong side of front, with white, Whipstitch short edges together; Overcast unfinished edges of front. For mouth, Overcast edges of D pieces, tacking pieces together at one short edge as you work. Glue snout, cheeks, mouth, ears and 12-mm cabochons to head as shown in photo.

NOTE: Cut one 6" circle of broadcloth and one 1" x 9" strip of gingham.

4: Substituting 6" circle for 12" circle and 1" x 9" strip for 2" x 24" strip, follow Step 7 of Cookie Jar. Insert head top into hatband as shown and glue to secure.❋

– Designed by Vicki Blizzard

A – Magnet Head
(cut 1) 16 x 18 holes

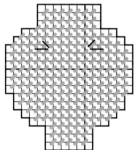

C – Magnet Snout Piece
(cut 4) 4 x 5 holes

E – Magnet Cheek
(cut 2)
4 x 4 holes

F – Magnet Ear
(cut 2) 5 x 6 holes

Whipstitch Y
edges together.

A – Menu Board
Head Front & Backing
(cut 1 each) 35 x 36 holes
Whipstitch between arrows.

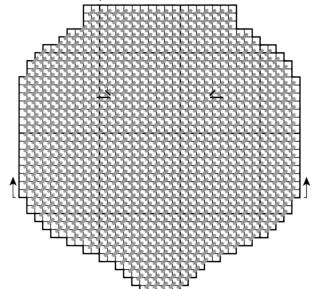

C – Menu Board
Snout Front
(cut 1) 11 x 14 holes

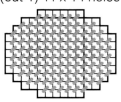

E – Menu Board
Mouth Piece
(cut 2)
4 x 10 holes

Whipstitch

Glue to head.

K – Menu
Board Hoof
(cut 4) 11 x 11 holes

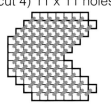

I – Menu Board
Spatula
(cut 1) 11 x 32 holes

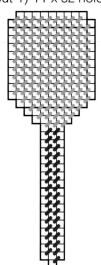

J – Menu Board
Spoon
(cut 1) 11 x 32 holes

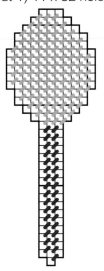

COLOR KEY: Chef Piggy

#3 pearl cotton or floss			AMOUNT
Med. Brown			12 yds.
Dk. Brown			5 yds.
Black			4 yds.
Metallic cord			**AMOUNT**
Silver			26 yds.

Worsted-weight	Nylon Plus™	Need-loft®	YARN AMOUNT
Pink	#11	#07	3$\frac{1}{2}$ oz.
White	#01	#41	87 yds.
Black	#02	#00	17 yds.
Lt. Pink	#10	#08	3 yds.
Maple	#35	#13	2 yds.

STITCH KEY:

— Backstitch/Straight Stitch
○ Bib Bead Attachment

L – Menu Board
Letters & Punctuation
(cut 1 each)
Cut out lt. green areas carefully.

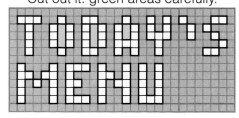

Chalk Holder
Assembly Diagram

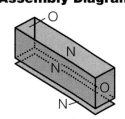

M – Menu Board
Tail Piece
(cut 2) 10 x 12 holes

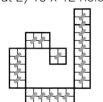

Fill zip-close bags with dry goods or treats and store inside these four adorable quilt-look containers.

Rustic Lodge Canisters

SIZE: Tree is 7" square x 9½" tall; Moon is 6" square x 8½" tall; Heart is 5¾" square x 7½" tall; Star is 5¼" square x 6½" tall.

SKILL LEVEL: Average

MATERIALS: Four sheets of 5-count plastic canvas; Two sheets of red 9" x 12" felt; Craft glue or glue gun; 44"-wide cotton or cotton/polyester fabric (for amounts see Color Key on page 91).

CUTTING INSTRUCTIONS:

NOTE: Graphs & diagrams on pages 90 & 91.

A: For Tree sides, cut four 29 x 45 holes.

B: For Tree lid top, cut one 33 x 33 holes.

C: For Tree lid sides, cut four 5 x 33 holes.

D: For Tree bottom, cut one 29 x 29 holes (no graph).

E: For Moon sides, cut four 25 x 40 holes.

F: For Moon lid top, cut one 29 x 29 holes.

G: For Moon lid sides, cut four 5 x 29 holes.

H: For Moon bottom, cut one 25 x 25 holes (no graph).

I: For Heart sides, cut four 23 x 35 holes.

J: For Heart lid top, cut one 27 x 27 holes.

K: For Heart lid sides, cut four 5 x 27 holes.

L: For Heart bottom, cut one 23 x 23 holes (no graph).

M: For Star sides, cut four 21 x 30 holes.

N: For Star lid top, cut one 25 x 25 holes.

O: For Star lid sides, cut four 5 x 25 holes.

P: For Star bottom, cut one 21 x 21 holes (no graph).

FABRIC PREPARATION INSTRUCTIONS:

NOTE: If desired, prewash fabric in cool water.

1: For fabric strips, measuring along one selvage edge of fabric, mark every ¾" and snip with sharp scissors to begin tear. (If selvage will not tear easily, trim off with scissors before snipping.)

2: Holding fabric firmly with both hands, starting at cut, tear into strips. Discard first and last strips if not correct width. Remove any long threads from strips.

STITCHING INSTRUCTIONS:

NOTES: To thread needle, fold one short end of strip in half and slide through eye of needle. Handle strips carefully to prevent excessive fraying.

Continued on page 90

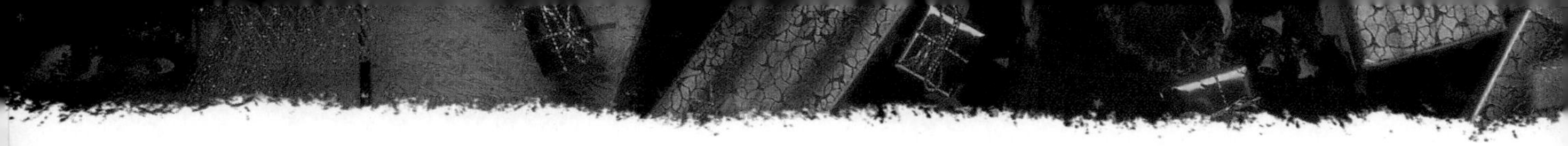

Bougainvillea Frame

Continued from page 78

E: For leaves, cut thirteen according to graph.

STITCHING INSTRUCTIONS:

1: Using colors and stitches indicated, work pieces (leave uncoded area of B unworked) according to graphs and stitch pattern guide. With matching colors, Overcast cutout edges of A and edges of E pieces.

NOTE: Cut one 6" length of white.

2: With white, Whipstitch and assemble A-C pieces, 6" strand, cardboard and acrylic glass as indicated on graphs and according to Frame Assembly Diagram.

3: For each flower (make 10), with red, Whipstitch three D pieces together as indicated and according to Flower Assembly Diagram; Overcast unfinished edges. For each flower center (make 10), assemble three stamens, three flower beads and one 1½" wire according to Flower Center Assembly Diagram.

4: Glue one flower center inside each flower (see photo). Arrange and glue flowers and leaves to front of Frame as desired or as shown in photo.❄

– Designed by Patricia Hall

COLOR KEY: Bougainvillea Frame

	Worsted-weight	Nylon Plus™	Need-loft®	YARN AMOUNT
▨	White	#01	#41	84 yds.
■	Red	#19	#02	60 yds.
▨	Green	#58	#28	22 yds.

STITCH KEY:

☐ Unworked Area/Support Attachment

Frame Assembly Diagram

(Back view; pieces are shown in different colors for contrast.)

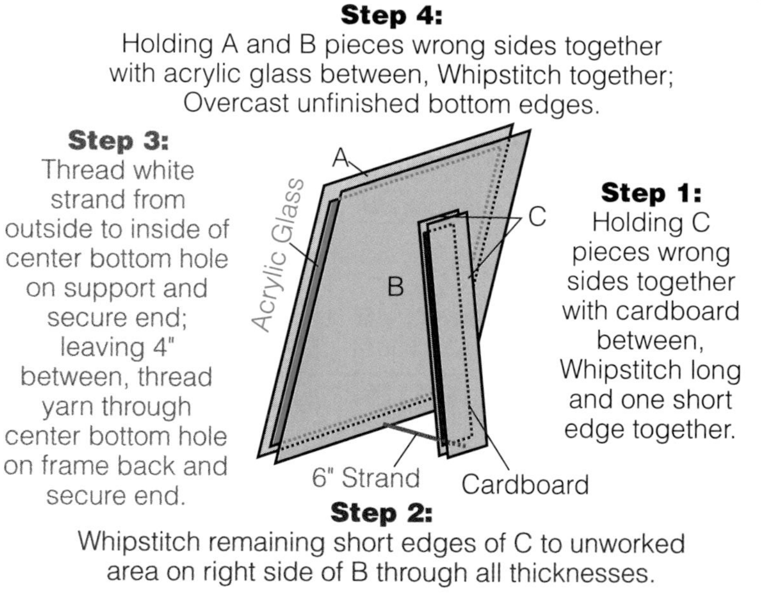
Step 4:
Holding A and B pieces wrong sides together with acrylic glass between, Whipstitch together; Overcast unfinished bottom edges.
Step 3:
Thread white strand from outside to inside of center bottom hole on support and secure end; leaving 4" between, thread yarn through center bottom hole on frame back and secure end.
A
Acrylic Glass
B
C
Step 1:
Holding C pieces wrong sides together with cardboard between, Whipstitch long and one short edge together.
6" Strand
Cardboard
Step 2:
Whipstitch remaining short edges of C to unworked area on right side of B through all thicknesses.

Flower Assembly Diagram

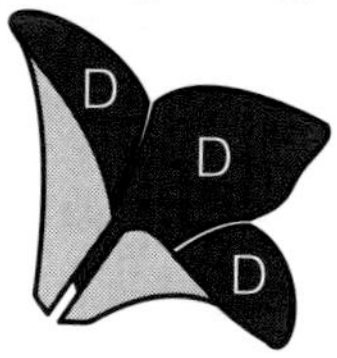
D
D
D

Back Stitch Pattern Guide

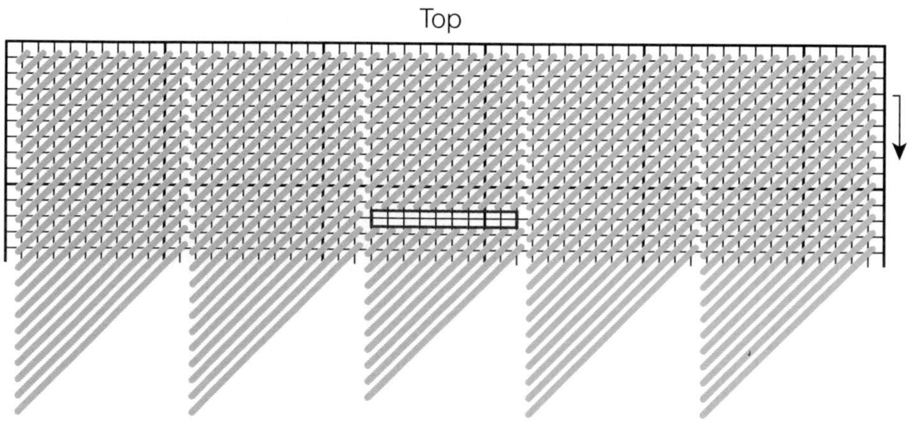
Top

Continue established pattern across entire piece.

Flower Center Assembly Diagram

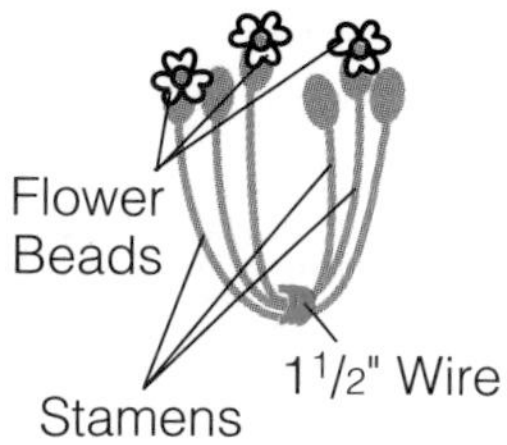
Flower Beads
Stamens
1 1/2" Wire

Nutcracker Soldier

Instructions & photo on pages 80 & 81

COLOR KEY: Nutcracker Soldier

	Worsted-weight	Nylon Plus™	Need-loft®	YARN AMOUNT
■	Royal	#09	#32	36 yds.
■	Black	#02	#00	10 yds.
▨	Lt. Pink	#10	#08	6¹/₂ yds.
■	Red	#19	#02	6 yds.
▨	Yellow	#26	#57	5 yds.
▨	White	#01	#41	4 yds.
■	Pink	#11	#07	¹/₂ yd.

STITCH KEY:

— Backstitch/Straight Stitch

A – Side
(cut 4) 30 x 36 holes

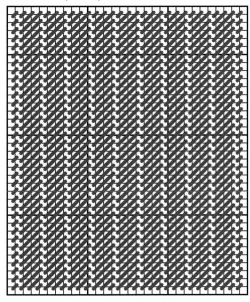

E – Face
(cut 1) 12 x 24 holes

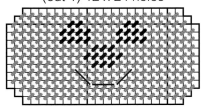

D – Plume
(cut 1)
7 x 7 holes

I – Arm
(cut 2)
7 x 12 holes

J – Hand
(cut 2)
5 x 5 holes

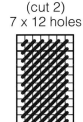

K – Epaulet
(cut 2)
4 x 9 holes

L – Foot
(cut 2)
4 x 13 holes

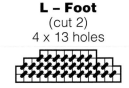

F – Left Side Hair
(cut 1)
9 x 12 holes

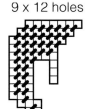

G – Right Side Hair
(cut 1)
9 x 12 holes

H – Straps
(cut 1)
16 x 30 holes

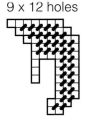

Tiny Tree Trimmings

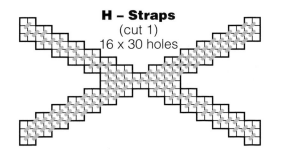

HOLIDAY PICK-ME-UP – Give a special friend a tiny tree decorated with soothing, fragrant, flavored teas and coffees.

• Secure tree trunk in decorative teapot, pack tissue paper around base inside teapot.

• Tie on individual tea bags, hot chocolate packages or coffee packets.

• Tuck in gift certificates for a facial or massage. Include home-made gift certificates for child care, house cleaning or a home cooked meal.

• Glue ribbon hangers on sample-size lotions and bath beads; hang on tree. Adorn tree top with lace bow and drape lace streamers vertically down through tree branches.

Christmas Spirit

Celestial Messengers

SIZE: Each is 1" x 3¼" x 4½", not including hangers.

SKILL LEVEL: Average

MATERIALS: One sheet of 10-count plastic canvas; Two 16-mm wooden doll heads; ½ yd. red ⅛" satin ribbon; Two white 2½" craft feathers; Two green 3½" cotton terry stems; Six red glass seed beads; Blonde mini-curl doll hair; Craft glue or glue gun; Medium metallic braid or metallic cord (for amount see Color Key); #3 pearl cotton or six-strand embroidery floss (for amounts see Color Key; double amounts for floss).

CUTTING INSTRUCTIONS:

A: For Red Angel dress, cut one according to graph.

B: For Green Angel dress, cut one according to graph.

STITCHING INSTRUCTIONS:

1: Using pearl cotton or twelve strands floss in colors and stitches indicated, work pieces according to graphs. Using braid or cord in colors and embroidery stitches indicated, embroider detail as indicated on graphs.

NOTE: Cut one 9" length each of dk. red and dk. green.

2: For each Angel, thread ends of one 9" strand from front to back over ✦ bar on corresponding dress as indicated; knot ends together on wrong side to secure. Folding dress wrong sides together as indicated, with matching color, Whipstitch together as indicated; Over-

A – Red Angel Dress
(cut 1)
37 x 42 holes

Whipstitch between arrows.

Whipstitch between arrows.

Fold Line

B – Green Angel Dress
(cut 1)
37 x 42 holes

Whipstitch between arrows

Fold Line

Whipstitch between arrows.

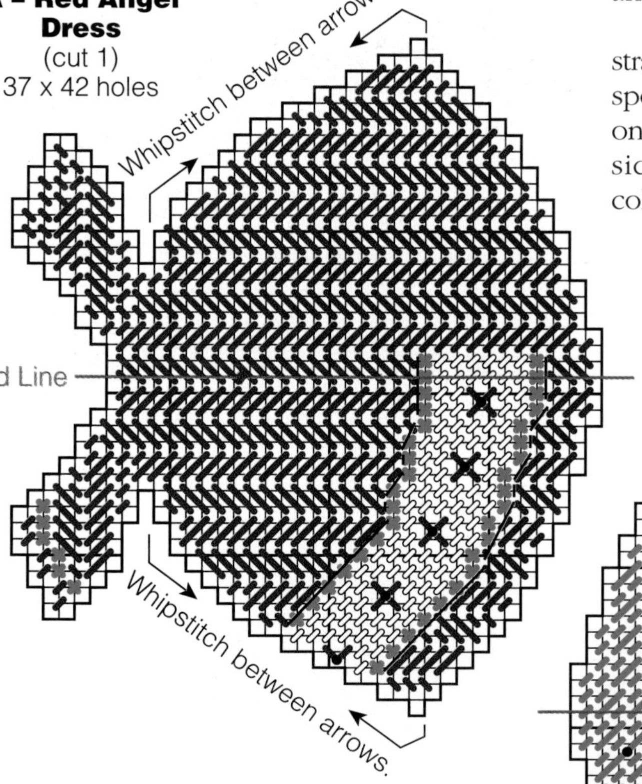

COLOR KEY: Celestial Messengers

Med. metallic braid or cord	AMOUNT
■ Gold	3 yds.

#3 pearl cotton or floss	AMOUNT
■ Dk. Red	20 yds.
■ Dk. Green	18 yds.
▨ White	6 yds.

STITCH KEY:
- — Backstitch/Straight Stitch
- • French Knot
- ✦ Hanger Attachment

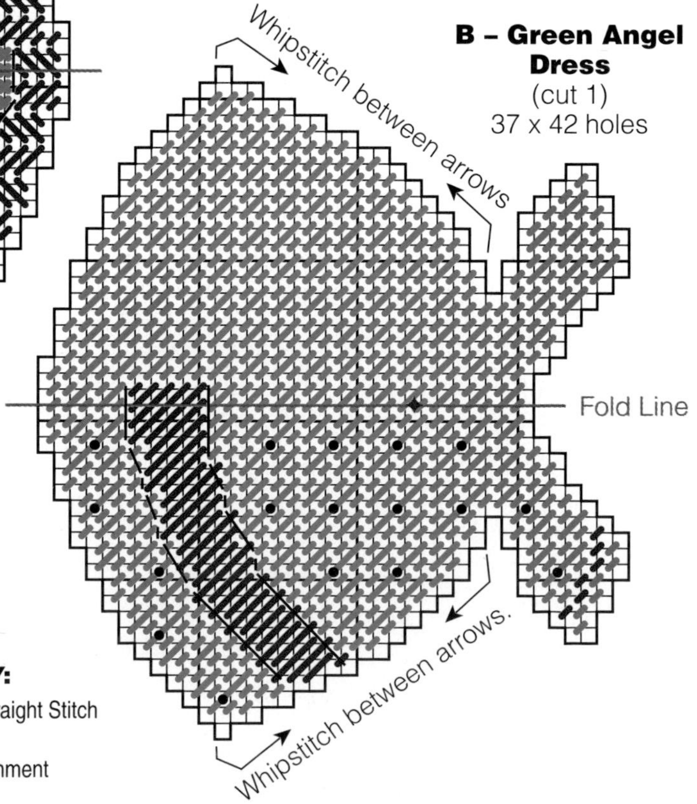

cast unfinished edges.

NOTE: Cut ribbon in half; tie each ribbon into a bow and trim ends as desired.

3: For each wreath, coil one terry stem twice to form a dime-sized wreath (see photo); glue three seed beads and one bow to wreath as shown in photo.

4: Glue one doll head, one feather for wings and one wreath to each dress as shown; glue a small amount of doll hair to each head as shown.✻

– Designed by Dianne Davis

Angelic Doorstop

SIZE: 2¾" x 5⅝" x 9" tall; holds a 2½" x 3½" x 7" brick or other weight.

SKILL LEVEL: Easy

MATERIALS: Two sheets of 7-count plastic canvas; 2½" x 3½" x 7" brick or a zip-close bag filled with gravel or other weighting material; 6" of light brown doll hair; Seasonal sprig of artificial holly leaves, berries and pine cones; Craft glue or glue gun; #3 pearl cotton or six-strand embroidery floss (for amounts see Color Key); Metallic cord (for amounts see Color Key); Worsted-weight or plastic canvas yarn (for amounts see Color Key).

CUTTING INSTRUCTIONS:

A: For angel, cut one according to graph.

B: For angel arms #1 and #2, cut one each according to graphs.

C: For angel wings #1 and #2, cut one each according to graph.

D: For Cover front and back, cut two (one for front and one for back) 26 x 51 holes (no graph).

E: For Cover top and bottom, cut two (one for top and one for bottom) 16 x 26 holes (no graph).

F: For Cover sides, cut two 16 x 51 holes (no graph).

STITCHING INSTRUCTIONS:

1: Using colors indicated and Continental Stitch, work A-

Cover Stitch Pattern Guide

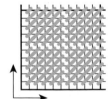

Continue established pattern up and across each entire piece.

C pieces according to graphs. With gold cord for angel's halo and with matching colors, Overcast edges of A-C pieces.

2: Using pearl cotton or six strands floss and embroidery stitches indicated, embroider facial detail on A as indicated on graph.

3: For Cover, using sea green and Scotch Stitch over five bars, work D-F pieces according to Cover Stitch Pattern Guide. With sea green, Whipstitch D-F pieces together, inserting weight before closing.

4: Tie a small amount of cord around center of hair. Gently pull hair apart to fluff; trim ends to even. Glue hair and arms to front of angel and holly sprig to hands as shown in photo. Glue wings to back of angel as shown. Matching bottom edges, glue angel to Cover.❈

– Designed by Michele Wilcox

COLOR KEY: Angelic Doorstop

#3 pearl cotton			AMOUNT
■ Dk. Blue			¼ yd.
■ Dk. Pink			¼ yd.
Metallic cord			**AMOUNT**
■ White/Gold			8 yds.
■ Blue/Silver			2 yds.

Worsted-weight	Nylon Plus™	Need-loft®	YARN AMOUNT
■ Sea Green	#37	#53	54 yds.
▨ White	#01	#41	10 yds.
■ Lemon	#25	#20	6 yds.
■ Dusty Rose	#52	#06	3 yds.
■ Coral	–	#65	3 yds.

STITCH KEY:
— Backstitch/Straight Stitch
● French Knot

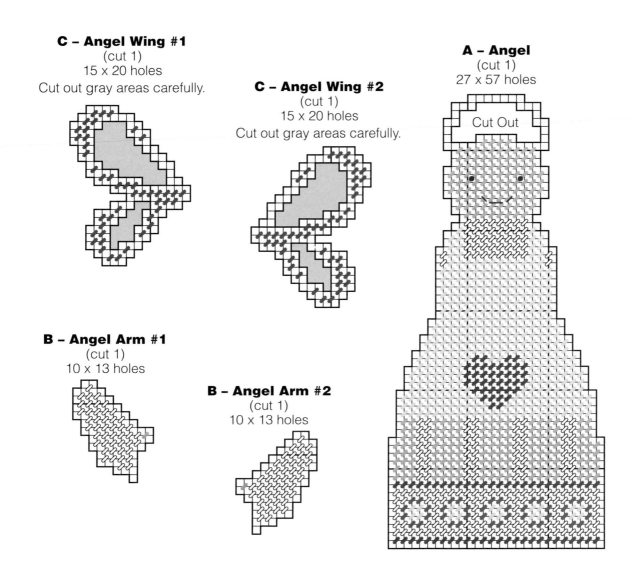

C – Angel Wing #1
(cut 1)
15 x 20 holes
Cut out gray areas carefully.

C – Angel Wing #2
(cut 1)
15 x 20 holes
Cut out gray areas carefully.

A – Angel
(cut 1)
27 x 57 holes

Cut Out

B – Angel Arm #1
(cut 1)
10 x 13 holes

B – Angel Arm #2
(cut 1)
10 x 13 holes

Musical Spirits

SIZE: Angel With Horn is 6½" x 10¾"; Angel With Harp is 6¾" x 8".

SKILL LEVEL: Easy

MATERIALS: One sheet of 7-count plastic canvas; Basket of choice; 2 yds. off-white 2⅝" and pink 1½" decorative ribbon; Craft glue or glue gun; Heavy metallic braid or metallic cord (for amounts see Color Key); Worsted-weight or plastic canvas yarn (for amounts see Color Key).

CUTTING INSTRUCTIONS:

A: For Angel With Horn, cut one according to graph.

B: For Angel with Harp, cut one according to graph on page 105.

STITCHING INSTRUCTIONS:

NOTE: Use doubled strand of braid or cord for stitching and a single strand for embroidery and Overcast.

1: Using colors and stitches indicated, work pieces according to graphs.

2: With braid or cord color to match dress color (see photo), gold braid or cord for wings and with matching colors as shown in photo, Overcast edges of A and B pieces. (**NOTE:** Do not Overcast harp strings on B.)

3: Using braid or cord in colors and embroidery stitches indicated, embroider hair and dress detail on A and B pieces as indicated on graphs.

4: Adorn basket with ribbons as desired or as shown in photo; glue angels to basket over ribbons as desired or as shown. ✳

– Designed by Trina Taylor Burch

COLOR KEY: Musical Spirits

Hvy. metallic braid or cord			AMOUNT
■ Gold			20 yds.
■ Blue			5 yds.
■ Pink			5 yds.

Worsted-weight	Nylon Plus™	Need-loft®	YARN AMOUNT
■ Lt. Blue	#05	#36	10 yds.
■ Rose	#12	#05	9 yds.
■ Tan	#33	#18	5 yds.
■ Eggshell	#24	#39	3 yds.
■ Lt. Pink	#10	#08	2 yds.

STITCH KEY:

— Backstitch/Straight Stitch

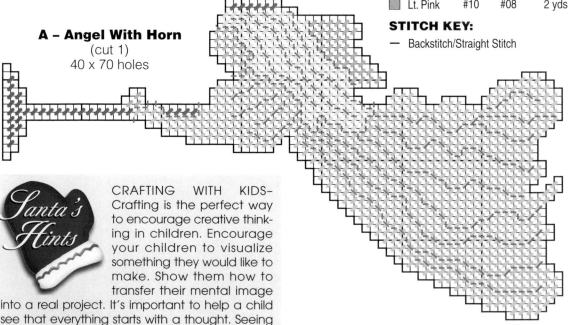

A – Angel With Horn
(cut 1)
40 x 70 holes

Santa's Hints

CRAFTING WITH KIDS–
Crafting is the perfect way to encourage creative thinking in children. Encourage your children to visualize something they would like to make. Show them how to transfer their mental image into a real project. It's important to help a child see that everything starts with a thought. Seeing the end result reinforces a self confidence that can translate into other areas of their life.

Make a joyful noise when you adorn a basket with heavenly angels.

Capture the color and majesty of an historic cathedral in this handy carry-all.

Stained Glass Tote

SIZE: 4¼" x 9" x 9" tall, not including handles.

SKILL LEVEL: Average

MATERIALS: 2¾ sheets of clear 7-count plastic canvas; 2½ sheets of white 7-count plastic canvas; One 3" plastic canvas radial circle; One magenta 27-mm acrylic faceted round stone; Craft glue or glue gun; Metallic cord (for amounts see Color Key); Worsted-weight or plastic canvas yarn (for amount see Color Key).

CUTTING INSTRUCTIONS:

NOTE: Graphs continued on pages 104 & 105.

A: For Tote front and lining, cut two (one from clear for front and one from white for lining) 59 x 59 holes.

B: For Tote back and lining, cut two (one from clear for back and one from white for lining) 59 x 59 holes.

C: For Tote sides and linings, cut four (two from clear for sides and two from white for linings) 24 x 59 holes.

D: For bottom, cut one from clear 24 x 59 holes (no graph).

E: For handles, cut two from clear 4 x 75 holes.

F: For cross, cut one from clear according to graph.

G: For cross support, use 3" circle.

STITCHING INSTRUCTIONS:

NOTE: D and lining A-C pieces are not worked.

1: Using colors and stitches indicated and leaving uncoded area of A unworked, work A-C and E-G pieces according to graphs. With gold, Overcast edges of F and G pieces and long edges of E pieces.

2: Using gold and Straight Stitch, embroider detail on front A as indicated on graph.

Continued on page 104

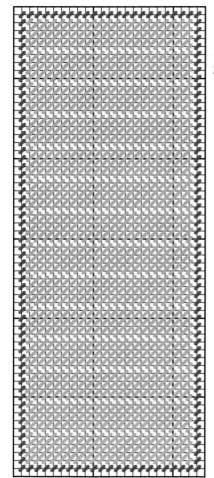

C – Side & Lining
(cut 2 from each color)
24 x 59 holes

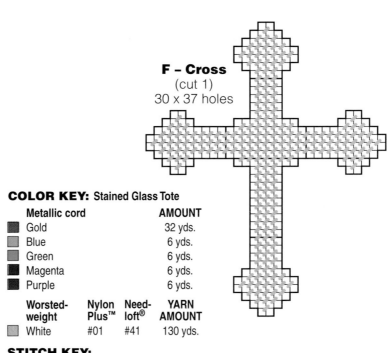

F – Cross
(cut 1)
30 x 37 holes

COLOR KEY: Stained Glass Tote

Metallic cord			AMOUNT
■ Gold			32 yds.
▨ Blue			6 yds.
▨ Green			6 yds.
■ Magenta			6 yds.
■ Purple			6 yds.

Worsted-weight	Nylon Plus™	Need-loft®	YARN AMOUNT
▨ White	#01	#41	130 yds.

STITCH KEY:

— Backstitch/Straight Stitch

Stained Glass Tote

Continued from page 103

3: Holding lining pieces to wrong side of corresponding worked pieces, with white, Whipstitch A-D pieces together through all thicknesses as needed to join; Whipstitch unfinished top edges together, catching ends of one handle to front and ends of remaining handle to back as indicated as you work.

4: Glue stone to cross, cross to support and support to Tote front as shown in photo.✻

– Designed by Debby Keel

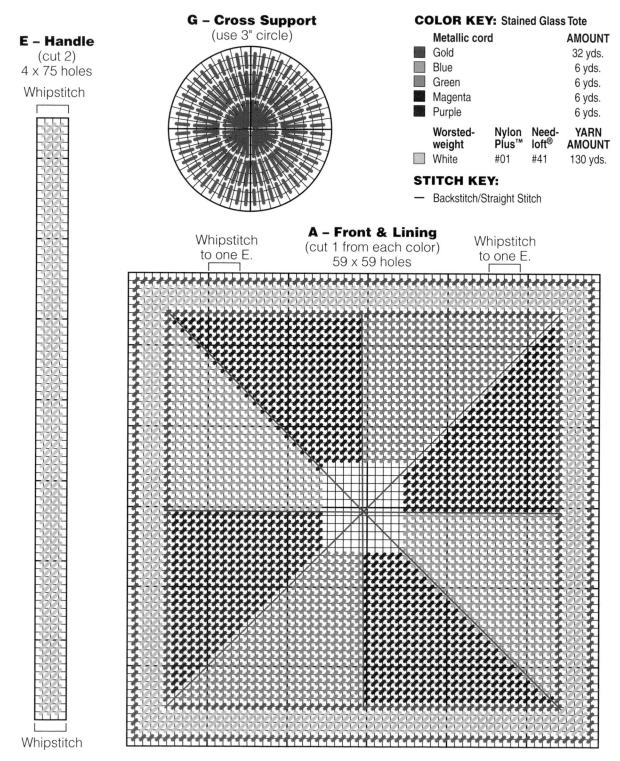

E – Handle
(cut 2)
4 x 75 holes

Whipstitch

Whipstitch

G – Cross Support
(use 3" circle)

Whipstitch to one E.

A – Front & Lining
(cut 1 from each color)
59 x 59 holes

Whipstitch to one E.

COLOR KEY: Stained Glass Tote

Metallic cord			AMOUNT
Gold			32 yds.
Blue			6 yds.
Green			6 yds.
Magenta			6 yds.
Purple			6 yds.

Worsted-weight	Nylon Plus™	Need-loft®	YARN AMOUNT
White	#01	#41	130 yds.

STITCH KEY:

— Backstitch/Straight Stitch

B – Back & Lining
(cut 1 from each color)
59 x 59 holes

Whipstitch to one E.

Whipstitch to one E.

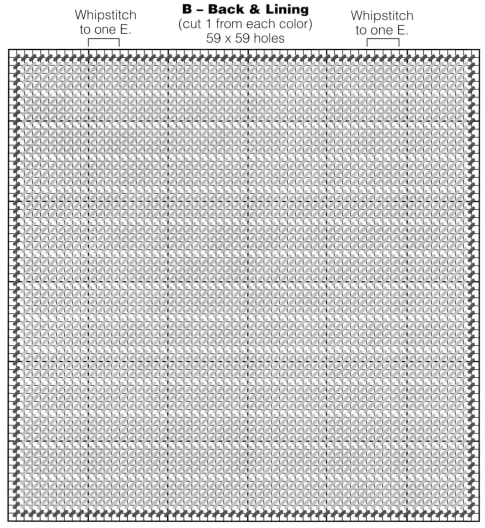

Musical Spirits

Instructions & photo on pages 100 & 101

B – Angel With Harp
(cut 1)
42 x 54 holes

Cut out gray areas carefully.

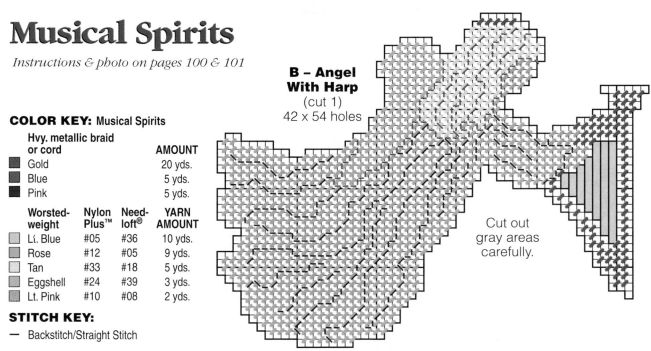

COLOR KEY: Musical Spirits

Hvy. metallic braid or cord			AMOUNT
Gold			20 yds.
Blue			5 yds.
Pink			5 yds.

Worsted-weight	Nylon Plus™	Need-loft®	YARN AMOUNT
Li. Blue	#05	#36	10 yds.
Rose	#12	#05	9 yds.
Tan	#33	#18	5 yds.
Eggshell	#24	#39	3 yds.
Lt. Pink	#10	#08	2 yds.

STITCH KEY:

— Backstitch/Straight Stitch

Bejeweled Angel

SIZE: 8½" across x 10" tall.

SKILL LEVEL: Challenging

MATERIALS: 1½ sheets of 7-count plastic canvas; Three green 20-mm and two of each red, blue and purple 12-mm foil-backed acrylic heart stones; Assorted sizes and types of gold trims; One 3" plastic angel doll head and two arms; Polyester fiberfill; Craft glue or glue gun; Metallic cord (for amount see Color Key); Worsted-weight or plastic canvas yarn (for amount see Color Key).

CUTTING INSTRUCTIONS:

NOTE: Graphs continued on pages 110 & 111.

A: For skirt, cut one according to graph.

B: For bodice front, cut one according to graph.

C: For bodice back, cut one according to graph.

D: For sleeves #1 and #2, cut one each according to graphs.

E: For wing tops, cut two according to graph.

F: For wing feathers, cut six according to graph.

STITCHING INSTRUCTIONS:

1: Using colors and stitches indicated, work pieces according to graphs. With cord, Overcast edges of E and F pieces.

2: For skirt, holding edges of A wrong sides togeth-

Top your tree with this richly dressed angel of serenity.

E – Wing Top
(cut 2)
12 x 12 holes

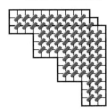

er, with dk. aqua, Whipstitch together as indicated on graph; Overcast unfinished edges.

3: Holding wrong sides together, with dk. aqua, Whipstitch Y edges of B together as indicated; repeat with C. Holding B and C pieces wrong sides together, Whipstitch side seams together as indicated, forming bodice; Overcast unfinished edges.

4: For each sleeve, holding cutout edges of one D right sides together, with dk. aqua, Whipstitch together (see Dart Illustration on page 111); holding underarm seams wrong sides together, Whipstitch together as indicated. Holding wrong sides together, Whipstitch X edges together at top of sleeve, forming shoulder seam; Whipstitch Y edges together at bottom, forming cuff. Overcast unfinished edges of sleeve.

5: Place doll head inside bodice; with back of bodice centered over back seam of skirt (see Bodice & Skirt Assembly Diagram on page 111), glue pieces together.

6: Push one doll arm through each sleeve and pull hand and arm through cuff (see photo); if desired, glue to secure. If desired, stuff sleeves with fiberfill to fluff; glue arms to bodice sides as shown in photo.

7: For each wing, glue right side of three feathers to wrong side of one wing top; glue right side of wing top to back of doll at shoulder blades (see photo).

8: Glue trims around skirt, waist, sleeve cuffs and bodice front as desired (see photo), trimming away excess as needed to fit. Glue one large and three small heart stones to right side of each wing top (see photo). Glue desired trim around back of remaining heart stone; glue stone to skirt front as shown. Glue ends of a 5" piece of trim together, forming halo; glue halo to doll head as shown.✷

– Designed by Sandra Miller Maxfield and Jimmy & Jessie Lampin

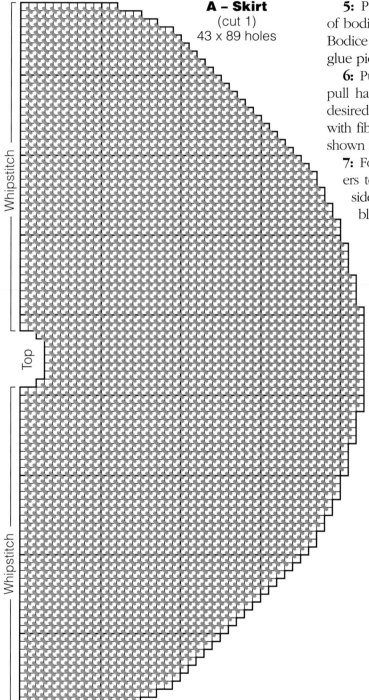

A – Skirt
(cut 1)
43 x 89 holes

Whipstitch

Top

Whipstitch

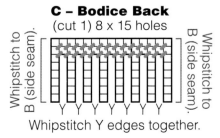

COLOR KEY: Bejeweled Angel

Metallic cord				AMOUNT
■ Gold				10 yds.

	Worsted-weight	Nylon Plus™	Need-loft®	YARN AMOUNT
■	Dk. Aqua	#08	#50	85 yds.

C – Bodice Back
(cut 1) 8 x 15 holes

Whipstitch to B (side seam).

Whipstitch to B (side seam).

Whipstitch Y edges together.

Christmas Advent Calendar

SIZE: 11" x 15⅜", not including hanger.

SKILL LEVEL: Average

MATERIALS: Two sheets of 7-count plastic canvas; One 9½" plastic canvas radial circle; One gold 1" round head brass-plated fastener; #5 pearl cotton or six-strand embroidery floss (for amount see Color Key); Metallic cord (for amount see Color Key); Worsted-weight or plastic canvas yarn (for amounts see Color Key).

CUTTING INSTRUCTIONS:

NOTE: Graphs continued on pages 110 & 111.

A: For calendar, cut one according to graph.

B: For angels #1 and #2, cut one each according to graphs.

C: For star, cut one according to graph.

D: For date wheel, cut one from 9½" circle according to graph.

STITCHING INSTRUCTIONS:

1: Using colors and stitches indicated and leaving uncoded center of D piece unworked, work pieces according to graphs. With matching colors as shown in photo, Overcast cutout edges of A and edges of B-D pieces. With

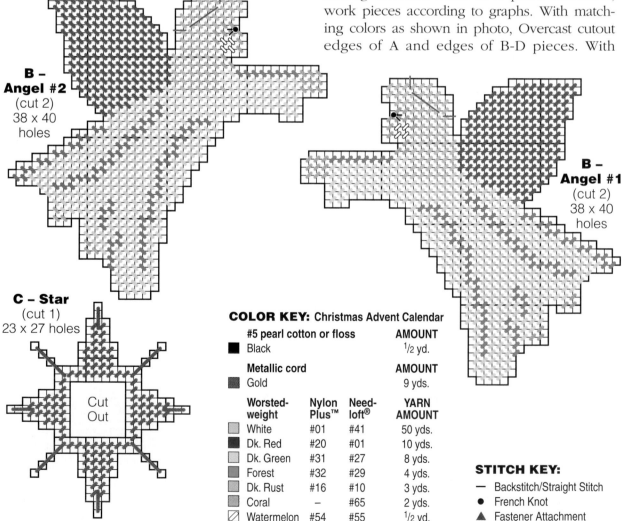

B – Angel #2
(cut 2)
38 x 40 holes

B – Angel #1
(cut 2)
38 x 40 holes

C – Star
(cut 1)
23 x 27 holes

Cut Out

COLOR KEY: Christmas Advent Calendar

#5 pearl cotton or floss			AMOUNT
■ Black			½ yd.

Metallic cord			AMOUNT
Gold			9 yds.

Worsted-weight	Nylon Plus™	Need-loft®	YARN AMOUNT
White	#01	#41	50 yds.
Dk. Red	#20	#01	10 yds.
Dk. Green	#31	#27	8 yds.
Forest	#32	#29	4 yds.
Dk. Rust	#16	#10	3 yds.
Coral	–	#65	2 yds.
▨ Watermelon	#54	#55	½ yd.

STITCH KEY:

— Backstitch/Straight Stitch

● French Knot

▲ Fastener Attachment

white, Overcast outer edges of A in every other hole (see photo); with dk. red, Overcast remaining outer edges.

2: Using pearl cotton or three strands floss, yarn and cord in colors and embroidery stitches indicated, embroider detail on A, B and D pieces as indicated on graphs.

3: Holding right side of D to wrong side of A, insert fastener from front to back through ▲ hole on A as indicated and through cutout of D, spread apart fastener ends at back to secure.

NOTE: Cut one 18" length each of white and red.

4: For hanger, twist 18" strands together; secure to corners of A. Glue C to A at matching cutouts as shown in photo; glue B pieces to A as shown.❋

– Designed by Cherie Marie Leck

Bejeweled Angel

Instructions & photo on page 106

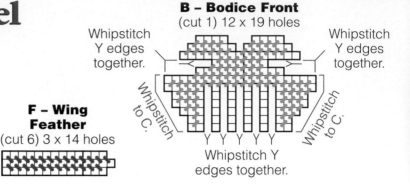

B – Bodice Front
(cut 1) 12 x 19 holes

Whipstitch Y edges together.

Whipstitch Y edges together.

Whipstitch to C.

Whipstitch to C.

Whipstitch Y edges together.

COLOR KEY: Bejeweled Angel

Metallic cord			AMOUNT
Gold			10 yds.

Worsted-weight	Nylon Plus™	Need-loft®	YARN AMOUNT
Dk. Aqua	#08	#50	85 yds.

F – Wing Feather
(cut 6) 3 x 14 holes

Christmas Advent Calendar

Instructions & photo on pages 108 & 109

Continue established pattern around entire circle.

D – Date Wheel
(cut 1 from 9¹/₂" circle)
Cut away gray center.

COLOR KEY: Advent Calendar

Metallic cord			AMOUNT
Gold			9 yds.

Worsted-weight	Nylon Plus™	Need-loft®	YARN AMOUNT
White	#01	#41	50 yds.
Dk. Red	#20	#01	10 yds.

STITCH KEY:

— Backstitch/Straight Stitch
▲ Fastener Attachment

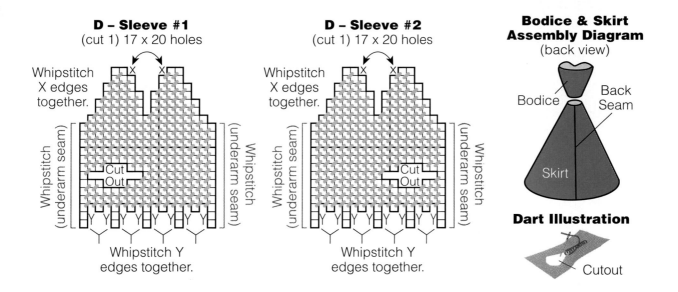

D – Sleeve #1
(cut 1) 17 x 20 holes

Whipstitch X edges together.

Whipstitch (underarm seam)

Cut Out

Whipstitch (underarm seam)

Whipstitch Y edges together.

D – Sleeve #2
(cut 1) 17 x 20 holes

Whipstitch X edges together.

Whipstitch (underarm seam)

Cut Out

Whipstitch (underarm seam)

Whipstitch Y edges together.

Bodice & Skirt Assembly Diagram
(back view)

Bodice

Back Seam

Skirt

Dart Illustration

Cutout

A – Calendar
(cut 1) 66 x 69 holes

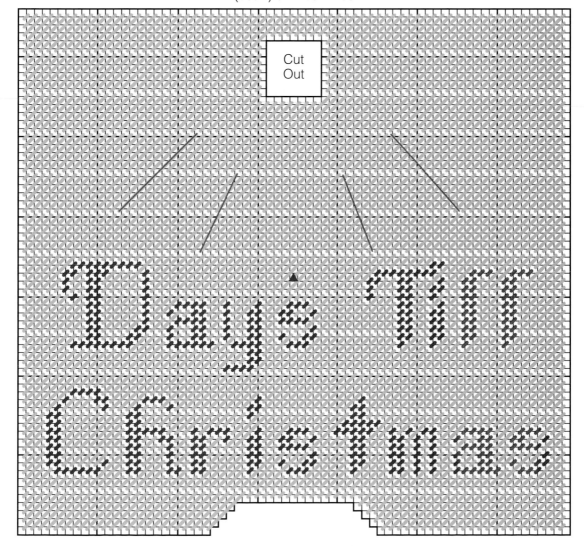

Cut Out

Santa Treats

Doorknob Basket

SIZE: $2\frac{5}{8}$" x $4\frac{5}{8}$" x $10\frac{1}{4}$".

SKILL LEVEL: Easy

MATERIALS: $\frac{3}{4}$ sheet of 7-count plastic canvas; One $4\frac{1}{2}$" plastic canvas radial circle; Raffia straw (for amounts see Color Key).

CUTTING INSTRUCTIONS:

A: For front, cut one 39 x 47 holes.

B: For back, cut one according to graph.

C: For bottom, cut one from circle according to graph on page 129.

STITCHING INSTRUCTIONS:

1: Using colors and stitches indicated and leaving uncoded areas of B unworked, work pieces according to graphs; with tan for basket handle and with red for top of basket back, Overcast cutout edges of B.

2: With matching colors, Whipstitch A-C pieces together as indicated on graphs and according to Basket Assembly Diagram; with red for front and with tan, Overcast unfinished edges.✳

– Designed by Nancy Marshall

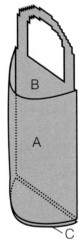

Basket Assembly Diagram

COLOR KEY: Doorknob Basket

Raffia straw	AMOUNT
Tan	30 yds.
Red	9 yds.
Green	3 yds.

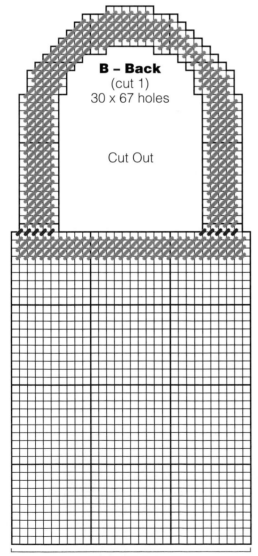

B – Back
(cut 1)
30 x 67 holes

Cut Out

Whipstitch to C.

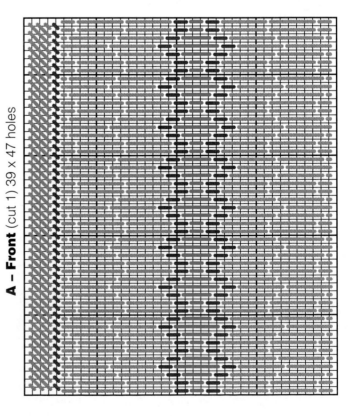

A – Front (cut 1) 39 x 47 holes

You'll be on your merry way with this handy catch-all for keys, sunglasses, etc.

Christmas Tic-Tac-Toe

SIZE: Box is 5½" square x 1½" tall; "X" game pieces are 1½" x 2"; "O" game pieces are 1½" x 1½".

SKILL LEVEL: Average

MATERIALS: One sheet of 7-count plastic canvas; Worsted-weight or plastic canvas yarn (for amounts see Color Key on page 119).

CUTTING INSTRUCTIONS:

NOTE: Graphs on page 119.

A: For lid top, cut one 36 x 36 holes.

B: For lid sides, cut three 3 x 36 holes.

C: For box sides, cut four 8 x 34 holes.

D: For "O" game pieces, cut five according to graph.

E: For "X" game pieces, cut five according to graph.

F: For box bottom, cut one 34 x 34 holes (no graph).

Continued on page 119

"X" and "O" mark the spot where holiday fun begins.

Organize your child's favorite toys in a colorful box built for easy toting and convenient storage between baths.

Bathtime Fun

SIZE: 8" x 13¾" x 6" tall, including handle.

SKILL LEVEL: Easy

MATERIALS: Four sheets of 7-count plastic canvas; Craft glue or glue gun; Worsted-weight or plastic canvas yarn; for amounts see Color Key on page 118.

CUTTING INSTRUCTIONS:

NOTE: Graphs on pages 118 & 119.

A: For sides, cut two 22 x 90 holes (no graph).

B: For ends, cut two 22 x 51 holes (no graph).

C: For bottom, cut one 51 x 90 holes (no graph).

D: For handle divider pieces, cut two according to graph.

E: For letters, cut number indicated accord-*Continued on page 118*

Bathtime Fun

Continued from page 117

Continued from page 117

ing to graphs.

STITCHING INSTRUCTIONS:

NOTE: C piece is not worked.

1: Using colors and stitches indicated, work D (leave uncoded area unworked) and E pieces according to graphs; using blue for sides, green for ends and Continental Stitch, work A and B pieces. With yellow, Overcast edges of E pieces.

2: Whipstitch A–D pieces together according to Caddy Assembly Diagram.

3: Glue letters to one side as shown in photo.✼

– Designed by Betty Radla

COLOR KEY: Bathtime Fun

	Worsted-weight	Nylon Plus™	Need-loft®	YARN AMOUNT
☐	Royal	#09	#32	60 yds.
☐	Green	#58	#28	40 yds.
■	Red	#19	#02	22 yds.
▨	Yellow	#26	#57	10 yds.

D – Handle Divider Piece (cut 2) 38 x 90 holes

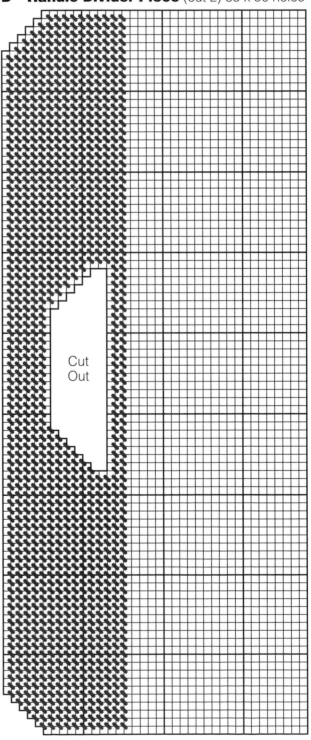

E – Letter "B"
(cut 1)
9 x 13 holes

E – Letter "A"
(cut 1)
9 x 13 holes

Caddy Assembly Diagram

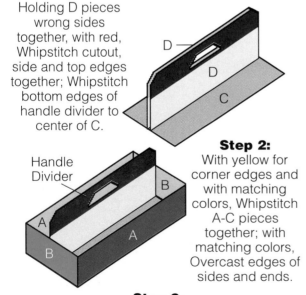

Step 1:
Holding D pieces wrong sides together, with red, Whipstitch cutout, side and top edges together; Whipstitch bottom edges of handle divider to center of C.

Handle Divider

Step 2:
With yellow for corner edges and with matching colors, Whipstitch A–C pieces together; with matching colors, Overcast edges of sides and ends.

Step 3:
Glue side edges of handle divider to ends.

E – Letter "H"
(cut 1)
9 x 13 holes

E – Letter "T"
(cut 2)
9 x 13 holes

E – Letter "O"
(cut 1)
9 x 13 holes

E – Letter "Y"
(cut 1)
9 x 13 holes

E – Letter "S"
(cut 1)
9 x 13 holes

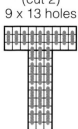
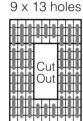
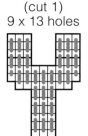
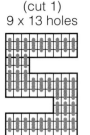

Christmas Tic-Tac-Toe *Continued from page 116*

STITCHING INSTRUCTIONS:

NOTE: F piece is not worked.

1: Using colors and stitches indicated, work A-E pieces according to graphs; fill in uncoded areas of A, D and E pieces using white and Continental Stitch. With dk. red for "X" pieces and with matching colors, Overcast D and E pieces.

2: With matching colors, Whipstitch A-C and F pieces together according to Box Assembly Diagram; with matching colors, Overcast unfinished edges of box and lid.

NOTE: Separate remaining red into 2-ply or nylon plastic canvas yarn into 1-ply strands.

3: Using 2-ply (or 1-ply) red and French Knot, embroider detail on "O" game pieces as indicated on graph.✳

– Designed by Cherie Marie Leck

COLOR KEY: Christmas Tic-Tac-Toe

Worsted-weight	Nylon Plus™	Need-loft®	YARN AMOUNT
■ Dk. Red	#20	#01	36 yds.
▨ Dk. Green	#31	#27	28 yds.
□ White	#01	#41	18 yds.

STITCH KEY:

● French Knot

A – Lid Top (cut 1) 36 x 36 holes

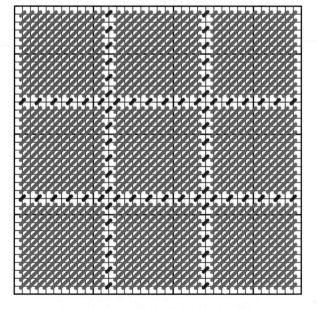

Box Assembly Diagram

(Pieces are shown in different colors for contrast.)

Step 1:
Whipstitch C and F pieces together.

Step 2:
Whipstitch A and B pieces together; Whipstitch A to one C.

D – "O" Game Piece
(cut 5) 9 x 9 holes

Cut Out

E – "X" Game Piece
(cut 5) 9 x 12 holes

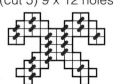

B – Lid Side (cut 3) 3 x 36 holes

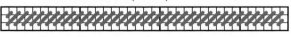

C – Box Side (cut 4) 8 x 34 holes

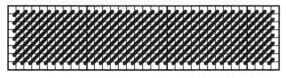

Clown Collector

SIZE: Loosely covers a boutique-style tissue box.

SKILL LEVEL: Challenging

MATERIALS: 2½ sheets of 7-count plastic canvas; Two 3" plastic canvas radial circles; Red curly doll hair; Polyester fiberfill; Craft glue or glue gun; #3 pearl cotton or six-strand embroidery floss (for amounts see Color Key on page 126); Worsted-weight or plastic canvas yarn (for amounts see Color Key).

CUTTING INSTRUCTIONS:

NOTE: Graphs & diagrams on pages 126-128.

A: For pocket, cut one according to graph.

B: For box sides, cut four 31 x 36 holes (no graph).

C: For box top, cut one according to graph.

D: For head pieces, cut two according to graph.

E: For head side pieces, cut two 7 x 24 holes (no graph).

F: For arm pieces, cut four according to graph.

G: For hand pieces, cut four according to graph.

H: For ear pieces, cut four according to graph.

I: For neck sides, cut two 5 x 7 holes (no graph).

J: For eyes #1 and #2 and mouth, cut one each according to graphs.

K: For eyebrows, cut two according to graph.

L: For suspenders, cut two 4 x 79 holes (no graph)

M: For neck band, cut one 4 x 58 holes (no graph).

N: For bow tie, cut one according to graph.

O: For nose, buttons and bow tie knot, cut number indicated according to graphs.

P: For shoe pieces, cut four according to graph.

Q: For hat crown, cut one 8 x 41 holes (no graph).

R: For hat brim, cut one from one 3" circle according to graph.

S: For hatband, cut one 2 x 47 holes (no graph).

T: For hat top and lining, cut two (one from remainder of cut circle for top and one from complete circle for lining) according to graph.

STITCHING INSTRUCTIONS:

1: Using colors and stitches indicated, work A-C, G (two on opposite side of canvas), H (two on opposite side of canvas), J, N, O (one for nose, three for shirt buttons and one for bow tie knot), P, R and T pieces according to graphs and stitch pattern guide; fill uncoded areas and work D-F (two F pieces on opposite side of canvas) and I pieces using white and Continental Stitch.

2: Using red for suspenders, orange for neck band, green for hat crown, yellow for hatband and Continental Stitch, work L, M, Q and S pieces. Substituting orange, purple, red, green and yellow for royal, work remaining O pieces for additional buttons according to graph. With red for mouth, white for eyes, royal for eyebrows and with matching colors, Overcast edges of J-l, long edges of M and N and O pieces. With yellow, Whipstitch ends of S together; Overcast edges of hatband.

3: Using pearl cotton colors indicated (use red and yellow for buttons as desired) and embroidery stitches indicated, embroider detail on eye J pieces, N and buttons as indicated on graphs.

NOTE: Cut two 10" lengths of red pearl cotton.

4: For each shoe top (make two), beginning at one top corner of cross stitch and leaving a 2½" tail on right side of work, using one 10" strand of red pearl cotton and embroidery stitches indicated, embroider shoe lacing on one P piece as indicated on graph, ending with a tail at top corner opposite beginning tail; tie tail ends into a bow.

5: For each shoe, holding one of each top and bottom P wrong sides together, with yellow, Whipstitch together.

6: For head, with white, Whipstitch D, E and I pieces together according to Head Assembly Diagram on page 127; Overcast unfinished top edges of head. Whipstitch neck edges to cutout edges on right side of C.

7: With royal, Whipstitch Y edges of A
Continued on page 126

From tissues to markers, this button-down guy gathers it all in one neat place.

Fill these elf-sized boxes with holiday goodies.

Christmas Candy Boxes

STOCKING CANDY BOX

SIZE: 1⅜" x 3½" x 4¼".

SKILL LEVEL: Average

MATERIALS: One sheet of 7-count plastic canvas; ¼ yd. each of white and red ⅛" satin ribbon; ¼ yd. white ½" gathered lace; 3" x 3" piece of clear acrylic glass; Craft glue or glue gun; Worsted-weight or plastic canvas yarn (for amounts see Color Key).

CUTTING INSTRUCTIONS:

A: For side #1, cut one according to graph.

B: For side #2, cut one according to graph.

C: For front, cut one 8 x 12 holes.

D: For toe, cut one 8 x 19 holes.

E: For bottom, cut one 8 x 15 holes.

F: For back/heel, cut one 8 x 26 holes.

G: For lid top, cut one 9 x 16 holes (no graph).

H: For lid long sides, cut two 5 x 16 holes (no graph).

I: For lid short sides, cut two 5 x 9 holes (no graph).

STITCHING INSTRUCTIONS:

1: Using red and Continental Stitch, work A-F pieces according to graphs; fill in uncoded areas and work G-I pieces using white and Continental Stitch.

NOTE: Using cutout area of B as pattern, cut one from acrylic glass ¼" larger at all edges.

2: Glue acrylic glass to wrong side of B over cutout.

3: With matching colors, Whipstitch A-F pieces together according to Stocking Box Assembly Diagram; with white, Whipstitch G and I pieces together, forming lid. With red for stocking and white for lid, Overcast unfinished edges.

4: Holding ribbons together, tie into a small bow; trim ends. Glue bow to one short side of lid; glue lace to inside edges of lid as shown in photo.

GIFT CANDY BOX

SIZE: 1⅝" x 3¾" x 5⅞" tall, including bow.
SKILL LEVEL: Average
MATERIALS: One sheet of 7-count plastic canvas; 3" x 3" piece of clear acrylic glass; Craft glue or glue gun; 4-ply yarn (for amount see Color Key on page 129); Worsted-weight or plastic canvas yarn (for amount see Color Key).

CUTTING INSTRUCTIONS:
NOTE: Graphs on page 129.
A: For front, cut one according to graph.
B: For back, cut one 23 x 26 holes.
C: For sides, cut two 9 x 26 holes.
D: For bottom, cut one 9 x 23 holes.
E: For lid top, cut one 10 x 24 holes.
F: For lid sides, cut two 4 x 24 holes.
G: For lid ends, cut two 4 x 10 holes.
H: For large bow loop, cut one 3 x 50 holes.
I: For small bow loops, cut two 3 x 22 holes.

STITCHING INSTRUCTIONS:
1: Using colors and stitches indicated, work pieces according to graphs; with Christmas variegated, Overcast cutout edges of A. With dk. green, Overcast long edges of H and I pieces.

2: Center and glue acrylic glass to wrong

Continued on page 129

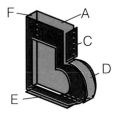

Stocking Box Assembly Diagram

(Pieces are shown in different colors for contrast.)

D – Stocking Toe
(cut 1)
8 x 19 holes
Whipstitch to C.

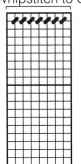

E – Stocking Bottom
(cut 1)
8 x 15 holes
Whipstitch to D.

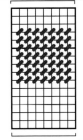

Whipstitch to F.

B – Stocking Side #2
(cut 1)
21 x 26 holes

Cut Out

COLOR KEY: Stocking Candy Box

	Worsted-weight	Nylon Plus™	Needloft®	YARN AMOUNT
■ Red		#19	#02	15 yds.
☐ White		#01	#41	13 yds.

C – Stocking Front
(cut 1)
8 x 12 holes

A – Stocking Side #1
(cut 1)
21 x 26 holes

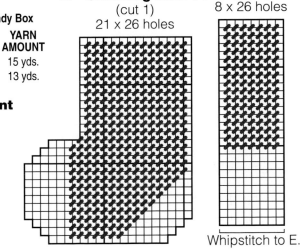

F – Stocking Back/Heel
(cut 1)
8 x 26 holes

Whipstitch to E.

Southern Belle

SIZE: Covers a standard-size roll of bathroom tissue.
SKILL LEVEL: Average
MATERIALS: One 13½" x 22½" sheet of 7-count plastic canvas; One 11½" fashion doll; 1 yd. white ⅜" satin ribbon; ½ yd. cream 1¼" gathered lace; Nine pink ½" ribbon roses; ¼ yd. white 3-mm pearl strand; Craft glue or glue

Add an air of romance to your bathroom with this clever cover-up.

gun; Worsted-weight or plastic canvas yarn (for amounts see Color Key).

CUTTING INSTRUCTIONS:
NOTE: Graphs continued on page 128.

A: For skirt, cut one according to graph.

B: For bodice front, cut one according to graph.

C: For bodice right side, cut one according to graph.

D: For bodice left side, cut one according to graph.

STITCHING INSTRUCTIONS:
NOTE: Do not remove doll's legs; they will fit into cardboard tube of tissue.

1: Using colors and stitches indicated, work A-D (overlap ends of A as indicated on graph and work through both thicknesses at overlap areas to join) pieces according to graphs.

2: Omitting dart seam above overlap seam, with pink, Whipstitch X edges of A together as indicated; Overcast straight top edges and bottom edge of skirt. Whipstitch and assemble A-D pieces as indicated and according to Skirt & Bodice Assembly Diagram on page 128.

3: Starting at back of skirt, glue straight edge of lace around skirt 1" from bottom edge (see photo); glue eight ribbon roses evenly spaced around top of lace and one rose to bodice front as indicated.

Continued on page 128

COLOR KEY: Southern Belle

Worsted-weight	Nylon Plus™	Need-loft®	YARN AMOUNT
■ Pink	#11	#07	52 yds.
▨ White	#01	#41	1 yd.

STITCH KEY:
▲ Rose Placement

A – Skirt (cut 1) 49 x 105 holes

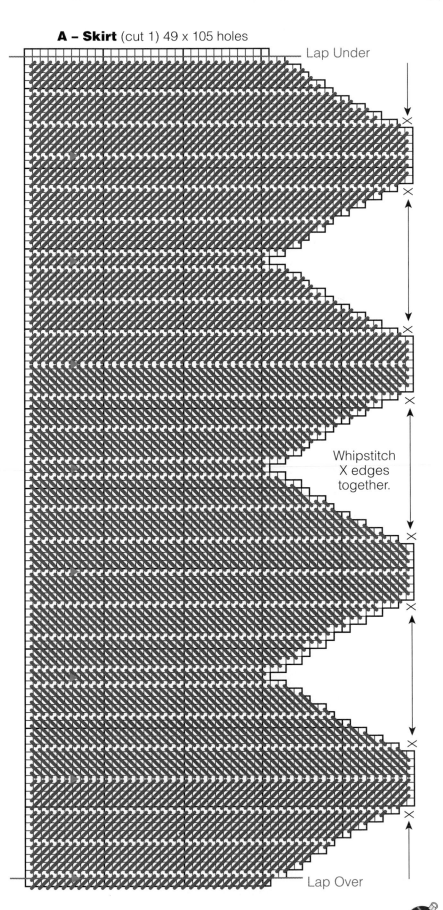

Lap Under

Whipstitch X edges together.

Lap Over

Clown Collector

Continued from page 120

together as indicated; Overcast top edge as indicated. Holding bottom edge of pocket even with bottom edge of one box side, with royal, Whipstitch bottom edges together. With matching colors, Whipstitch A-C pieces together through all thicknesses at pocket side edges. With royal, Overcast unfinished bottom edges of box.

8: For each arm, holding two F pieces wrong sides together, with white, Whipstitch together as indicated, stuffing with fiberfill as you work; Overcast unfinished edges. With green, Overcast edges of G pieces as indicated; for each hand, holding two G pieces wrong sides together, Whipstitch unfinished edges together. For each ear, with white, Whipstitch

two H pieces wrong sides together.

NOTE: Separate remaining white into 2-ply or nylon plastic canvas yarn into 1-ply strands.

9: Using 2-ply (or 1-ply) white and Straight Stitch, embroider detail on eye J pieces and nose O as indicated.

10: Whipstitch and assemble Q-T pieces according to Hat Assembly Diagram on page 127.

11: Glue L pieces to box according to Suspender Placement Diagram on page 128; glue front ends of suspenders to pocket front as indicated, and glue one yellow button to each suspender as shown in photo. Glue hands inside arms and arms to box sides according to Arm Placement Diagram on page 127 (see photo).

12: Assemble M, N and knot O pieces according to Bow Tie Assembly Diagram on page 128. Slide tie assembly over head; glue bottom of tie to top front of box between suspenders as shown.

13: Glue shoes to bottom front edge of box; glue ears to head as indicated and facial features, hair and hat to head as shown. Glue royal buttons to front of box as shown; glue remaining buttons to hat, arms, box top and back as shown or as desired.

14: Place assembly over tissue box and pull tissues out through hat. Fill front pocket and hands with art supplies as desired.❋

– Designed by Vicki Blizzard

C – Box Top (cut 1) 31 x 31 holes

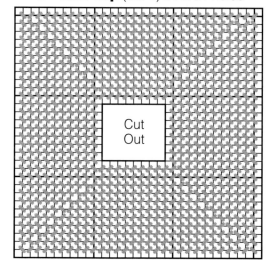

Cut Out

H – Ear Piece
(cut 4)
3 x 6 holes

Glue to head side.

A – Pocket
(cut 1) 19 x 39 holes

Overcast

Whipstitch to B.

Whipstitch to B.

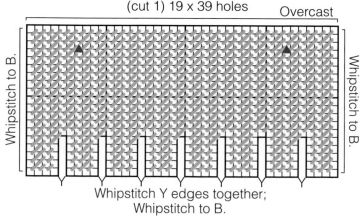

Whipstitch Y edges together;
Whipstitch to B.

COLOR KEY: Clown Collector

#3 pearl cotton or floss			AMOUNT
■ Yellow			6 yds.
■ Red			4 yds.
■ Black			1 yd.

Worsted-weight	Nylon Plus™	Need-loft®	YARN AMOUNT
White	#01	#41	85 yds.
Royal	#09	#32	64 yds.
Green	#58	#28	18 yds.
Red	#19	#02	24 yds.
Yellow	#26	#57	10 yds.
Orange	#17	#58	9 yds.
Purple	#21	#46	2 yds.
Black	#02	#00	1 yd.

STITCH KEY:
- — Backstitch/Straight Stitch
- ● French Knot
- × Cross Stitch
- ▲ Suspender Placement

D – Head Piece
(cut 2) 17 x 25 holes

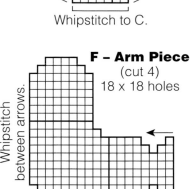

Whipstitch to one E between arrows.

Whipstitch to one E between arrows.

Whipstitch to C.

F – Arm Piece
(cut 4)
18 x 18 holes

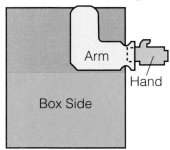

Whipstitch between arrows.

G – Hand Piece
(cut 4)
7 x 11 holes

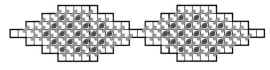

Overcast

K – Eyebrow
(cut 2)
3 x 5 holes

J – Eye #1
(cut 1)
4 x 5 holes

J – Eye #2
(cut 1)
4 x 5 holes

J – Mouth
(cut 1)
4 x 5 holes

O – Bow Tie Knot
(cut 1)
4 x 4 holes

P – Shoe Piece
(cut 4)
7 x 12 holes

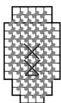

N – Bow Tie
(cut 1) 7 x 32 holes

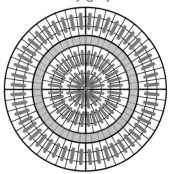

O – Button
(cut 28)
4 x 4 holes

O – Nose
(cut 1)
4 x 4 holes

R – Hat Brim
(cut 1 from 3" circle)
Cut away gray area.

Box Side Stitch Pattern Guide

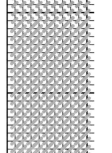

Continue established pattern across each entire piece.

T – Hat Top & Lining
(cut 1 each)

Arm Placement Diagram

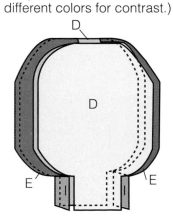

Arm

Hand

Box Side

Head Assembly Diagram
(Pieces are shown in different colors for contrast.)

D

D

E   E

Hat Assembly Diagram

Step 1:
With green, Whipstitch short ends of Q together; Whipstitch Q to cutout edge of R.

Step 2:
Overcast unfinished edges of Q and R.

Step 3:
Slip S over hat assembly.

Step 4:
For hat top, Whipstitch T pieces wrong sides together.

Step 5:
Tack one edge of hat top to one edge of Q.

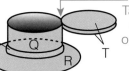

S   Q   T
R

Clown Collector

Instructions & photo on pages 120 & 121

Bow Tie Assembly Diagram
(Pieces are shown in different colors for contrast.)

Step 1:
Bring short ends of N to center; glue to secure.

Step 2:
Glue knot O over center of tie.

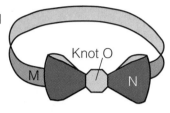

Step 3:
With orange, Whipstitch short ends of M together; glue bow tie assembly over band seam.

Suspender Placement Diagram
(Back view; some pieces are shown in different colors for contrast.)

Step 1:
Positioning one end of one L over pocket as indicated on A graph, glue to top of box.

Step 2:
Crossing pieces in back, repeat with remaining L; glue suspenders together and to back of box.

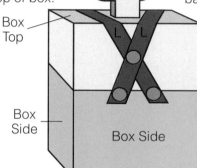

Head

Box Top

Box Side

Box Side

Step 3:
Glue three buttons to suspenders at back.

Southern Belle

Continued from page 125

NOTE: Cut one 1" and one 3" length of pearl strand; cut five individual pearls.

4: Glue 1" pearl strand around one wrist and 3" strand around neck; glue three pearls down bodice back for buttons and one pearl to each ear for earrings (see photo).

NOTE: Cut one 18" and one 9½" length of white satin ribbon.

5: Tie 18" ribbon into a bow around doll's waist for belt; use 9½" ribbon to embellish doll's hair as shown or as desired.✻

– Designed by Judy L. Nelson

Skirt & Bodice Assembly Diagram
(Back view; doll not shown for clarity.)

Step 1:
Omitting back seam, with pink, Whipstitch B-D pieces together; with matching colors, Overcast unfinished top and bottom edges.

Step 2:
Place bodice on doll; with pink, Whipstitch bodice back seam together.

Step 3:
Place skirt on doll with overlap seam at one side of back; Whipstitch final dart seam together.

B

D C

A

Overlap Seam

B – Bodice Front
(cut 1)
9 x 14 holes

Whipstitch to C.

Whipstitch to D.

C – Bodice Right Side
(cut 1)
12 x 13 holes

Back seam; Whipstitch to D.

Whipstitch to B between arrows.

D – Bodice Left Side
(cut 1)
12 x 13 holes

Whipstitch to B between arrows.

Back seam; Whipstitch to C.

COLOR KEY: Southern Belle

	Worsted-weight	Nylon Plus™	Need-loft®	YARN AMOUNT
■	Pink	#11	#07	52 yds.
■	White	#01	#41	1 yd.

STITCH KEY:
▲ Rose Placement

Christmas Candy Boxes *Continued from page 123*

side of front over cutout.

3: With Christmas variegated, Whipstitch A-D pieces together, forming box, and E-G pieces together, forming lid; Overcast unfinished edges of box and lid. With right side of work facing out, bring ends of H together at center; with dk.

green, Whipstitch together through all thicknesses as indicated on graph. Whipstitch ends of each I together.

4: Glue H and I pieces together to form bow as shown in photo; glue bow to lid.❈

– Designed by Joyce Keklock

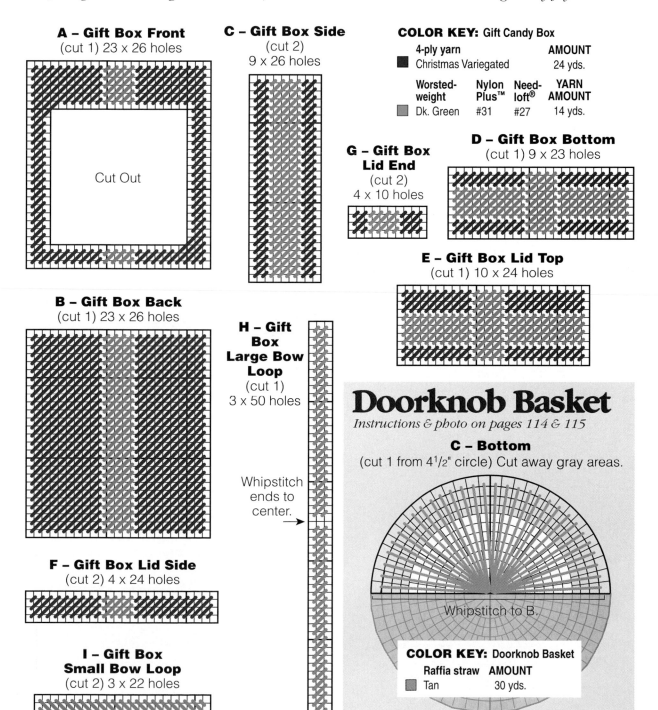

A – Gift Box Front
(cut 1) 23 x 26 holes

Cut Out

B – Gift Box Back
(cut 1) 23 x 26 holes

F – Gift Box Lid Side
(cut 2) 4 x 24 holes

**I – Gift Box
Small Bow Loop**
(cut 2) 3 x 22 holes

C – Gift Box Side
(cut 2)
9 x 26 holes

**H – Gift
Box
Large Bow
Loop**
(cut 1)
3 x 50 holes

Whipstitch
ends to
center. →

COLOR KEY: Gift Candy Box

4-ply yarn			AMOUNT
■ Christmas Variegated			24 yds.

Worsted-weight	Nylon Plus™	Need-loft®	YARN AMOUNT
■ Dk. Green	#31	#27	14 yds.

**G – Gift Box
Lid End**
(cut 2)
4 x 10 holes

D – Gift Box Bottom
(cut 1) 9 x 23 holes

E – Gift Box Lid Top
(cut 1) 10 x 24 holes

Doorknob Basket
Instructions & photo on pages 114 & 115

C – Bottom
(cut 1 from 4¹/₂" circle) Cut away gray areas.

Whipstitch to B.

COLOR KEY: Doorknob Basket

Raffia straw	AMOUNT
■ Tan	30 yds.

Happy
Holiday
Sea-Sun

Festive
Trimmings

Pretty Pinecones

SIZE: Each is 3½" across x 3" long, not including embellishments.

SKILL LEVEL: Challenging

MATERIALS FOR ONE: One sheet of 7-count plastic canvas; 1 yd. of ⅛" satin ribbon; One 3" - 5" artificial bird; Three or more artificial pine sprigs; Craft glue or glue gun; Worsted-weight or plastic canvas yarn (for amount see Color Key).

CUTTING INSTRUCTIONS:

A: For cone sections #1, cut two according to graph.

B: For cone sections #2, cut three according to graph.

C: For cone sections #3, cut four according to graph.

D: For cone sections #4, cut three according to graph.

STITCHING INSTRUCTIONS:

1: Using desired color and stitches indicated, work pieces according to graphs; Overcast outside edges of each piece.

2: Whipstitch and assemble ribbon and pieces according to Pinecone Assembly Diagram. Glue sprigs and bird to top as desired or as shown in photo.❋

– Designed by Robin Will

COLOR KEY: Pretty Pinecones

Worsted-weight	YARN AMOUNT
▨ Desired Color	22 yds.

A – Cone Section #1
(cut 2) 11 x 11 holes

Cut out gray area carefully.

B – Cone Section #2
(cut 3) 13 x 13 holes

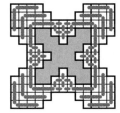

Cut out gray area carefully.

C – Cone Section #3
(cut 4) 15 x 15 holes

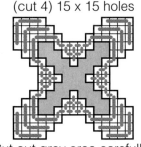

Cut out gray area carefully.

D – Cone Section #4
(cut 3) 17 x 17 holes

Cut out gray area carefully.

Pinecone Assembly Diagram
(Pieces are shown in different colors for contrast.)

Step 1:
For each section, holding right sides together, Whipstitch cutout edges together.

Cone Section

Step 2:
Fold ribbon in half and tie a knot 4" from fold, forming hanger.

4"

Step 3:
Thread each end of ribbon from back to front through center of each cone section in order shown.

Step 4:
Push sections together while pulling ribbon taught, then tie a knot close to last section to secure; trim ends of ribbon close to knot.

Step 5:
Hold top of assembly firmly in one hand and with other hand, turn sections in a clockwise direction.

Create a realistic-looking pinecone adorned with seasonal greenery for a delightful holiday centerpiece or ornament.

Elegant Snow Angels

SIZE: Each is 2" x 6⅜" x 7¾", not including hanger.

SKILL LEVEL: Average

MATERIALS: 1½ sheets of clear 7-count plastic canvas; ½ sheet of white 10-count plastic canvas; Four black 5-mm half-round beads; 10 silver 3-mm beads; Polyester fiberfill; ¼ yd. lt. blond wool doll hair; Craft glue or glue gun; Metallic cord (for amounts see Color Key); Worsted-weight or plastic canvas yarn (for amounts see Color Key).

CUTTING INSTRUCTIONS:

NOTES: Graphs continued on page 142.

Use white 10-count for E and clear 7-count canvas for remaining pieces.

A: For fronts, cut two according to graph.

B: For backs, cut two according to graph.

C: For wings, cut two according to graph.

D: For crowns, cut two according to graph.

E: For snowflake pieces, cut twenty according to graph.

STITCHING INSTRUCTIONS:

NOTE: E pieces are not worked.

1: Using colors and stitches indicated, work A-D (substitute pink cord for blue cord on one A, one B and one D) pieces according to graphs.

2: With matching colors, Overcast edges of C pieces and A pieces as indicated on graph. For each crown, with matching color, overlapping short ends of one D one hole as indicated and working through both thicknesses as one at overlap area to join, Whipstitch together; Overcast unfinished edges.

3: Using dusty rose and Backstitch, embroider facial detail on A pieces as indicated on graph.

4: For each Angel, holding wrong side of head, arms and upper dress area on back A to wrong side of front at matching edges, with matching colors, Whipstitch together as indicated; Overcast unfinished edges.

NOTE: Cut doll hair into four 3" lengths.

5: For each Angel, fold one length of hair over top of head so ends are at front and back;

COLOR KEY: Elegant Snow Angels

Metallic cord			AMOUNT
■ Blue			20 yds.
□ Pink			20 yds.

Worsted-weight	Nylon Plus™	Need-loft®	YARN AMOUNT
■ White	#01	#41	10 yds.
■ Orchid	#56	#44	7 yds.
■ Dusty Rose	#52	#06	1 yd.

STITCH KEY:

— Backstitch/Straight Stitch

O Eye Placement

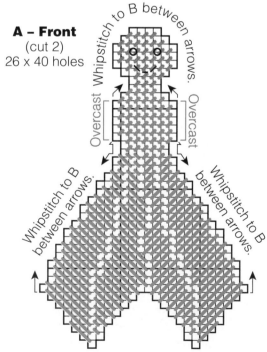

A – Front
(cut 2)
26 x 40 holes

Whipstitch to B between arrows.
Overcast Whipstitch to B between arrows. Overcast
Whipstitch to B between arrows.
Whipstitch to B between arrows.

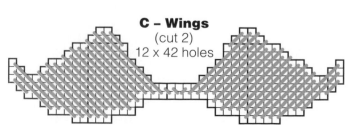

C – Wings
(cut 2)
12 x 42 holes

Create a winter wonderland as these lovely beings gently release snowflakes while flying high above the clouds.

glue at top to secure. Trim center ends at front for bangs and ends at back to desired length. Place one length of hair on each side of head; glue to secure. Trim ends to desired length. Gently pull hair apart to fluff.

6: Glue two beads to each face for eyes as indicated and matching wings and crown to each Angel as shown in photo. Gently fold arms of each Angel to front and glue hands together to secure.

7: For each snowflake (make 10), glue two E pieces and one silver bead together (see photo). Glue five snowflakes to each Angel as desired or as shown. Hang or display as desired.❊

– Designed by Robin Will

Lil' Package Ornaments

SIZE: Each is a 1⅞" cube.

SKILL LEVEL: Easy

MATERIALS FOR ONE: Scraps of 7-count plastic canvas; 1 yd. desired color ⅛" metallic ribbon or heavy metallic braid; Craft glue or glue gun (optional); Worsted-weight or plastic canvas yarn (for amounts see Color Key).

CUTTING INSTRUCTIONS:

A: For sides, cut six 11 x 11 holes (no graph).

STITCHING INSTRUCTIONS:

1: Using colors and stitches indicated, work pieces according to Side Stitch Pattern Guide of choice.

2: With main color, Whipstitch pieces together. Wrap metallic ribbon or cord around box and tie into a bow on one side (see photo); glue to secure, if desired.

3: Hang or display as desired.✢

– *Designed by Cherie Marie Leck*

COLOR KEY: Lil' Package Ornaments

Worsted-weight		YARN AMOUNT
■	Main Color	9 yds.
□	Contrasting Color	6 yds.

Side Stitch Pattern Guide #1	**Side Stitch Pattern Guide #2**	**Side Stitch Pattern Guide #3**	**Side Stitch Pattern Guide #4**
	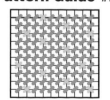	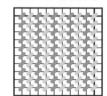	

Yuletide Warmers

SIZE: Each is 2⅞" x 4".

SKILL LEVEL: Easy

MATERIALS: ½ sheet of 7-count plastic canvas; 12" of 22-gauge wire; Pliers; Worsted-weight or plastic canvas yarn (for amounts see Color Key).

CUTTING INSTRUCTIONS:

A: For mitten #1, cut two according to graph.

B: For mitten #2, cut two according to graph.

STITCHING INSTRUCTIONS:

1: Using colors and stitches indicated, work pieces according to graphs. For each mitten, holding one of each A and B wrong sides together, with matching colors, Whipstitch together.

2: Thread one end of wire through ▲ holes on one mitten as indicated on graph; fold 1" of end up and with pliers, twist around wire (see photo). Repeat on opposite end of wire with remaining mitten. Bend wire to curve (see photo). Hang as desired.✻

– Designed by Nancy Marshall

COLOR KEY: Yuletide Warmers

	Worsted-weight	Nylon Plus™	Need-loft®	YARN AMOUNT
■	Red	#19	#02	8 yds.
■	White	#01	#41	8 yds.
■	Royal	#09	#32	5 yds.
■	Green	#58	#28	3 yds.

A – Mitten #1
(cut 2) 18 x 25 holes

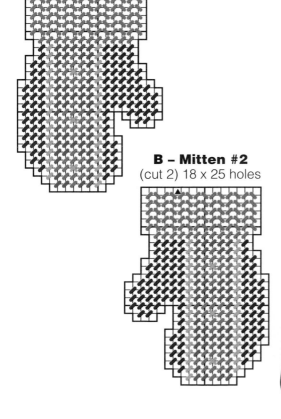

B – Mitten #2
(cut 2) 18 x 25 holes

Bring a bit of warmth inside with cozy mitten decorations.

Snowy Evergreen

SIZE: 10½" x 11¼".

SKILL LEVEL: Average

MATERIALS: Two sheets of 7-count plastic canvas; One set of 10 multicolor battery-operated musical twinkle lights; Two each red and white 12" chenille stems; 2 yds. red ⅛" satin ribbon; ⅔ yd. white 4-mm pearl strand; Self-adhesive closure strip; Craft glue or glue gun; Worsted-weight or plastic canvas yarn (for amounts see Color Key).

CUTTING INSTRUCTIONS:

A: For front, cut one according to graph.

B: For backing, cut one according to graph on page 143.

STITCHING INSTRUCTIONS:

NOTE: B piece is not worked.

1: Using colors and stitches indicated, work A according to graph.

2: For top garland, cut one 23-bead strand of pearls; break apart four pearls on each side and remove to expose floss. Starting at one end of strand and leaving a 2" tail, wrap satin ribbon in a spiral fashion between pearls to opposite end; leaving a 2" tail, cut away excess ribbon. Thread ends of ribbon and floss at each end of strand from front to back through top ▲ holes on A as indicated on graph and glue to back to secure.

3: For center garland, with a 35-bead strand, follow Step 2, gluing center of garland to front under cutout (see photo). For bottom garland, with a 50-bead strand, follow Step 2, gluing center of garland to front under cutout (see photo).

Continued on page 143

A – Front
(cut 1)
68 x 74 holes

Cut out gray areas carefully.

COLOR KEY: Snowy Evergreen

	Worsted-weight	Nylon Plus™	Needloft®	YARN AMOUNT
	White	#01	#41	21 yds.
	Forest	#32	#29	8 yds.
	Dk. Brown	#36	#15	2 yds.

Liven up the holiday season with a snow-covered tree adorned with blinking lights.

Add a sprinkle of magic to garlands or gift boxes with a trio of traditional ornaments.

Festive Touches

SIZE: Each is 2½" x 4".

SKILL LEVEL: Easy

MATERIALS: One sheet of 7-count plastic canvas; One gold 15-mm foil-backed acrylic star stone; 15 assorted color 5-mm foiled-backed acrylic round stones; Craft glue or glue gun; Metallic cord (for amounts see Color Key on page 142); Worsted-weight or plastic canvas yarn (for amounts see Color Key).

CUTTING INSTRUCTIONS:

NOTE: Graphs on pages 142 & 143.

A: For gift boxes, cut three 16 x 26 holes.

B: For candle, cut one according to graph.

C: For leaves, cut six according to graph.

D: For holly berry, cut one according to graph.

E: For poinsettia bracts, cut two according to graph.

F: For tree branches, cut one according to graph.

G: For tree trunk, cut one 3 x 7 holes.

STITCHING INSTRUCTIONS:

1: Using colors and stitches indicated, work

Continued on page 142

Christmas Candles

SIZE: Snugly covers a boutique-style tissue box.

SKILL LEVEL: Easy

MATERIALS: 1¼ sheets of 7-count plastic canvas; 20 assorted red and dk. pink ⅜"-½" decorative buttons; 2 yds. of dk. pink #3 pearl cotton or six-strand embroidery floss; Worsted-weight or plastic canvas yarn (for amounts see Color Key on page 153).

Continued on page 153

Festive Touches

Continued from page 140

pieces (substitute dk. red for red on one E) according to graphs. With metallic cord, Overcast edges of one A in each color; with orange for flame, dk. red for wax (see photo) and with matching colors, Overcast edges of B-G pieces.

2: Using gold cord and French Knot, embroider flower center on red E as indicated on graph.

3: Glue candle, two leaves and holly berry to gold/white gift box, poinsettia bracts and remaining leaves to green/white gift box, and tree branches and trunk to red/white gift box as shown in photo. Glue star stone to box at top of tree and round stone to tree branches as shown.

4: Hang as desired.✳

– Designed by Kimberly A. Suber

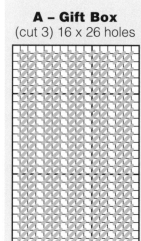

A – Gift Box
(cut 3) 16 x 26 holes

B – Candle
(cut 1)
5 x 22 holes

C – Leaf
(cut 6)
6 x 6 holes

D – Holly Berry
(cut 1)
2 x 2 holes

COLOR KEY: Festive Touches

Metallic cord			AMOUNT
Green			3 yds.
Red			3 yds.
Gold			3 yds.

Worsted-weight	Nylon Plus™	Need-loft®	YARN AMOUNT
Iridescent White	–	–	15 yds.
Red	#19	#02	5 yds.
Green	#58	#28	4 yds.
Dk. Green	#31	#27	4 yds.
Dk. Red	#20	#01	3 yds.
Cinnamon	#44	#14	1 yd.
Orange	#17	#58	1 yd.
Yellow	#26	#57	1 yd.

STITCH KEY:
- ● French Knot

Elegant Snow Angels

Instructions & photo on pages 134 & 135

COLOR KEY: Elegant Snow Angels

Metallic cord			AMOUNT
Blue			20 yds.
Pink			20 yds.

Worsted-weight	Nylon Plus™	Need-loft®	YARN AMOUNT
White	#01	#41	10 yds.
Orchid	#56	#44	7 yds.
Dusty Rose	#52	#06	1 yd.

STITCH KEY:
- — Backstitch/Straight Stitch
- O Eye Placement

D – Crown
(cut 2) 3 x 17 holes

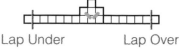

Lap Under   Lap Over

E – Snowflake Piece
(cut 20 from white 10-count)
5 x 5 holes

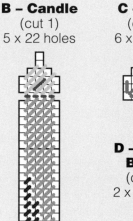

B – Back
(cut 2)
32 x 44 holes

Whipstitch to A between arrows.

Whipstitch to A between arrows.

Whipstitch to A between arrows.

Work area below dk. pink line on opposite side of canvas.

E – Poinsettia Bract
(cut 2) 11 x 11 holes

F – Tree Branches
(cut 1)
13 x 14 holes

G – Tree Trunk
(cut 1)
3 x 7 holes

Snowy Evergreen

Continued from page 138

4: Attach fuzzy side of closure to wrong side of A at area corresponding to cutout on B; glue loopy side to light switch box. Attach switch box to A and insert lights into cutouts. Holding backing to wrong side of front, with matching colors, Whipstitch together.

NOTE: Cut three 9" lengths of ribbon; cut six each 2¾" lengths of white and red chenille stems.

5: Tie each ribbon into a small bow; trim ends. For each candy cane, twist one of each color chenille stem together; bend one end to shape. Glue ribbons and candy canes to front as desired or as shown in photo. Hang as desired.✻

– Designed by Diane T. Ray

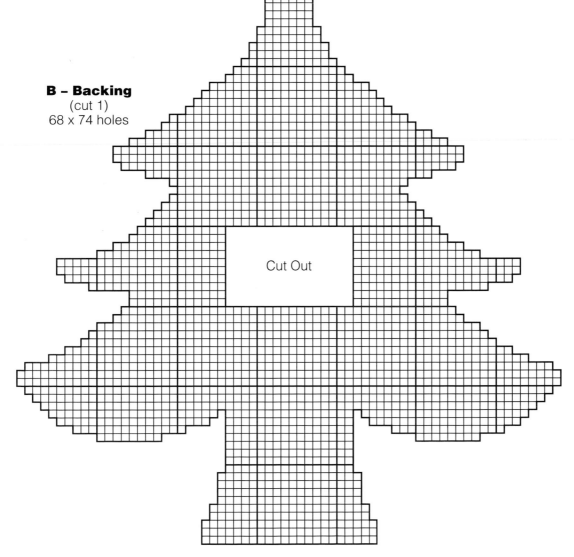

B – Backing
(cut 1)
68 x 74 holes

Cut Out

Shimmering Shapes

SIZE: Star Frame is 5½" across with a 3"-across photo window; Hexagon Frame is 5" across with a 2½"-across photo window; Gift Box Frame is 4¾" x 5½" with a 2⅝"-across photo window.

SKILL LEVEL: Average

MATERIALS: Two each Uniek® Crafts 5" plastic canvas star shapes and 6" hexagon shapes; ½ sheet of 7-count plastic canvas; Metallic cord (for amounts see Color Key).

CUTTING INSTRUCTIONS:

NOTE: Graphs continued on page 150.

A: For Star Frame front, cut one from one star shape according to graph; cut off hanger.

B: For Star Frame backing, use remaining star shape.

C: For Hexagon Frame front, cut one from one hexagon shape according to graph; cut off hanger.

D: For Hexagon Frame backing, use remaining hexagon shape.

E: For Gift Box Frame front and backing, cut two (one for front and one for backing) according to graph.

STITCHING INSTRUCTIONS:

NOTE: Backing pieces are not worked.

Wrapping Creatively

TISSUE ELEGANCE – Iron colored tissue paper and place on protected surface. Pour ¼ cup bleach in small bowl. Dip a toothbrush or a plastic mesh dish scrubber into bleach and dribble and flick onto paper. Allow to dry. Iron paper if desired. Wrap gift and tie tasseled cord in double knot around package.

1: Using colors and stitches indicated, work A, C and front E according to graphs; with gold, Overcast cutout edges.

2: For Star and Hexagon frames, holding backing to wrong side of matching front piece with hanger of backing piece at center top (see photo), with gold, Whipstitch together as indicated on graphs; Overcast unfinished edges of front.

3: For Gift Box Frame, holding backing E to wrong side of front, with gold, Whipstitch together as indicated; with gold for box and teal for bow (see photo), Overcast unfinished edges of front.

4: Hang as desired.✳

– Designed by Cherie Marie Leck

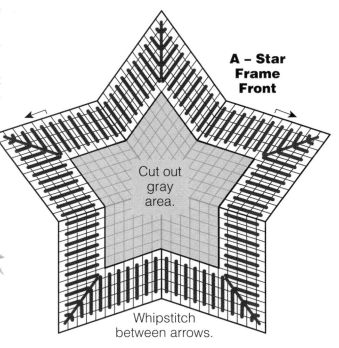

A – Star Frame Front

Cut out gray area.

Whipstitch between arrows.

COLOR KEY: Shimmering Shapes

	Metallic cord	AMOUNT
☐	Gold	9 yds.
■	Magenta	6 yds.
▨	Purple	6 yds.
▨	Teal	5 yds.

Spotlight the ones you love in three dazzling frame ornaments.

Celebrate the season in warmer climates with this sea-sun-al wreath adorned with starfish Santas, beach balls and festive ribbon.

Tropical Holiday Decor

SIZE: Decorates a 22"-wide wreath.

SKILL LEVEL: Average

MATERIALS: One 12" x 18" or larger sheet of 7-count plastic canvas; One sheet of 7-count plastic canvas; One 22"-wide artificial evergreen wreath; 7½ yds. Christmas plaid 2½" ribbon; 4¼ yds. of 22-gauge floral wire; Pliers or wire cutters; Three white ½" tinsel pom-poms; Five assorted color 1"-square decorative gift packages; Five assorted color 1"-wide decorative gift bows; Three red 5-mm foil-backed acrylic faceted round stones; Craft glue or glue gun; Six-strand embroidery floss (for amounts see Color Key on page 151); Pearlized metallic cord (for amount see Color Key); Worsted-weight or plastic canvas yarn (for amounts see Color Key).

CUTTING INSTRUCTIONS:

NOTE: Graphs on pages 151-153.

A: For wreath motif, cut one from large sheet according to graph.

B: For tree trunk, cut one according to graph.

C: For tree leaves, cut three according to graph.

D: For starfish Santas, cut three according to graph.

E: For starfish Santa hats, cut three according to graph.

F: For beach balls, cut three according to graph.

G: For basket front, cut one according to graph.

H: For basket back, cut one according to graph.

I: For basket bottom, cut one according to graph.

J: For basket trim, cut one 4 x 34 holes.

K: For basket handle, cut one 4 x 56 holes.

STITCHING INSTRUCTIONS:

NOTE: H and I pieces are not worked.

1: Using colors and stitches indicated, work A-G, J and K pieces according to graphs; fill in uncoded areas of A using red and Continental Stitch. With cinnamon for starfish Santas, white for basket handle and with matching colors, Overcast edges of B-F pieces, K, and one long edge of J. (**NOTE:** Do not Overcast edges of A.)

2: Using colors and embroidery stitches indicated, embroider facial detail on D pieces as indicated on graph.

3: Whipstitch and assemble G-K pieces as indicated and according to Basket Assembly Diagram on page 152.

NOTE: Cut one 2-yd. and one 3-yd. length of ribbon; cut one 18" length of wire.

4: Starting and ending at back, wrap 2-yd. ribbon around wreath (see photo). Glue or knot ends at back to secure; trim away excess ribbon. Shape 3-yd. ribbon into a multi-loop bow (see photo). With wire, attach bow to wreath, twisting wire ends together at back of wreath to secure.

NOTE: Cut seven 18" lengths of wire.

5: Thread one wire through canvas at center back of basket and place basket on front of wreath; wrap wire around wreath and twist ends together at back to secure. If desired, cut off excess wire. Thread one wire through yarn at center back of each starfish Santa and beach ball; attach pieces to wreath as for basket (see photo).

NOTE: Cut four 12" lengths of ribbon; cut one 9" length of wire.

6: For streamers, trim one end of each rib-
Continued on page 151

Tiny Tree Trimmings

GINGERBREAD TREE – Sweet gingerbread men dance on the branches of a mini tree.
• Secure tree trunk in cookie jar or recipe box.
• Use rick-rack or lace for garland. Or, thread hole candies on ribbon.
• Hang gingerbread cookies on tree with dental floss.
• Tie measuring spoons onto tree with ribbon.

Pearls & Lace

SIZE: Each is about 1¾" x 3⅛", not including trims.

SKILL LEVEL: Average

MATERIALS: One sheet of white 14-count plastic canvas; 1 yd. lavender ¹⁄₁₆" satin ribbon; 1 yd. lavender 4" tulle or netting; ½ yd. iridescent white ½" pre-gathered lace trim; ½-yd. strand of clear iridescent 2-mm plastic beads; 10 purple iridescent glass seed beads; Two crystal seed beads; Six 3-mm iridescent star sequins; Two 6-mm rondell crystal beads; One large floral stick pin; 3 yds. dk. green metallic blending filament; Sewing needle and white thread; Craft glue or glue gun; Six-strand embroidery floss (for amounts see Color Key).

CUTTING INSTRUCTIONS:

NOTE: Graphs continued on page 150.

A: For Boot front and back, cut two (one for front and one for back) according to graph.

B: For Glove front and back, cut two (one for front and one for back) according to graph.

C: For Tussie Mussie front and back, cut two (one for front and one for back) according to graph.

STITCHING INSTRUCTIONS:

NOTES: Back pieces are not worked.

Use six strands floss for solid colors; for blended colors, hold three strands floss and one strand blending filament together.

1: Using colors and stitches indicated, work one of each A-C piece for fronts according to graphs.

2: For each Ornament, holding back to wrong side of front, Whipstitch together as indicated on graphs; Overcast unfinished top edges.

NOTE: Cut one 2½" length each of lace and ribbon.

3: Holding ribbon and lace together at straight edges, with thread, sew ribbon, lace and purple seed beads together and to Boot through both thicknesses (see photo).

NOTE: Cut one 2¾" length each of lace and ribbon; cut one 3½" length of lace.

4: Holding 2¾" lace and ribbon together at straight edges, with thread, sew together around wrist edge of Glove (see photo); sew 3½" lace around inside top edge of glove as shown. Sew one crystal seed bead and one rondell bead together and to wrist lace of Glove (see photo).

NOTE: Cut one 2" and one 5" length of lace; cut one 6" length of ribbon.

5: With thread, sew 2" ribbon around point

A – Boot Front & Back
(cut 1 each) 26 x 43 holes

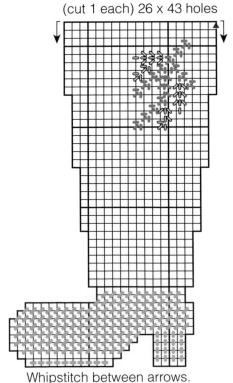

Whipstitch between arrows.

COLOR KEY: Pearls & Lace

Embroidery floss	AMOUNT
☐ White	9 yds.
▨ Gray	5 yds.
☐ Dk. Green	3 yds.
☐ Lt. Green	2 yds.
▦ Blended Dk. Green	
▨ Blended Lt. Green	

STITCH KEY:

▲ Hanger Attachment

of Tussie Mussie (see photo). Matching straight edges as shown, sew 5" ribbon around open edges of Tussie Mussie. Tie 6" ribbon into a bow; holding bow over lace at point, sew remaining crystal seed bead and rondell bead together and to point over bow to secure (see photo).

NOTE: Cut three 9" lengths each of pearl strand and ribbon.

6: For each hanger, thread each end of one ribbon through hole on one star sequin, then tie a knot in end of ribbon to secure. Fold ribbon in half and fold one pearl strand into a bow; holding ribbon and bow together, sew together and to edge of one Ornament as indicated (see photo).

NOTE: Cut tulle or netting into three equal pieces.

7: Fold one tulle or netting piece and insert into each Ornament, and insert stick pin into Tussie Mussie Ornament as shown.✳

– Designed by Rosemarie Walter

Pearls & Lace

Instructions & photo on pages 148 & 149

B – Glove Front & Back
(cut 1 each) 22 x 44 holes

C – Tussie Mussie Front & Back
(cut 1 each) 27 x 42 holes

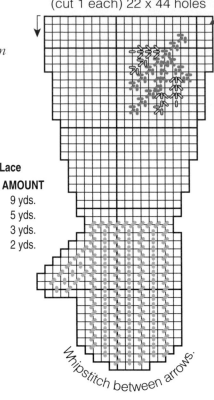

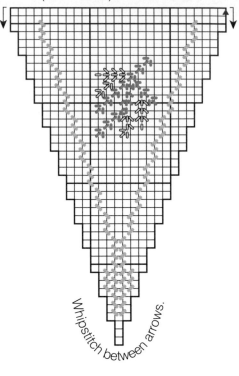

Whipstitch between arrows.

COLOR KEY: Pearls & Lace

Embroidery floss	AMOUNT
☐ White	9 yds.
▨ Gray	5 yds.
☐ Dk. Green	3 yds.
☐ Lt. Green	2 yds.
▨ Blended Dk. Green	
▨ Blended Lt. Green	

STITCH KEY:

▲ Hanger Attachment

Shimmering Shapes

Instructions & photo on page 144 & 145

COLOR KEY: Shimmering Shapes

Metallic cord	AMOUNT
☐ Gold	9 yds.
■ Magenta	6 yds.
■ Purple	6 yds.
▨ Teal	5 yds.

C – Hexagon Frame Front

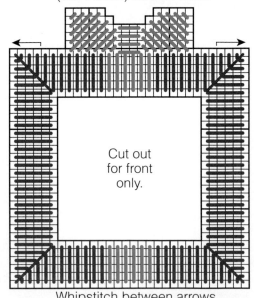

Whipstitch between arrows.

Cut out gray area.

E – Gift Box Frame Front & Backing
(cut 1 each) 30 x 35 holes

Cut out for front only.

Whipstitch between arrows.

Tropical Holiday Decor

Continued from page 147

bon as desired (see photo). Poke wire through opposite end of each ribbon; secure wire to center bottom of wreath (see photo), twisting ends together at back to secure.

7: Glue tree trunk and leaves to A and red stones to leaves (see photo). Holding right side of A to back of wreath, glue, or with scraps of yarn, tack A to wreath to secure.

NOTE: Cut four 9" lengths of ribbon. Trim three ribbons to ⅛"-wide and remaining ribbon to ¾"-wide.

8: Tie each ribbon into a bow; trim ends as desired. Glue one small bow and one hat to each starfish Santa, and one pom-pom to tip of each hat as shown. Glue large bow to basket, package ornaments to inside of basket as

shown, and bows to packages and beach balls (see photo).❋

– Designed by Glenda Chamberlain

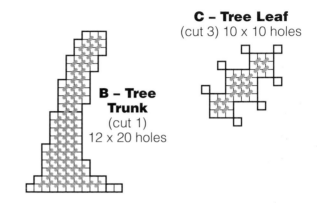

C – Tree Leaf
(cut 3) 10 x 10 holes

B – Tree Trunk
(cut 1)
12 x 20 holes

E – Starfish Santa Hat
(cut 3)
8 x 10 holes

K – Basket Handle
(cut 1)
4 x 56 holes

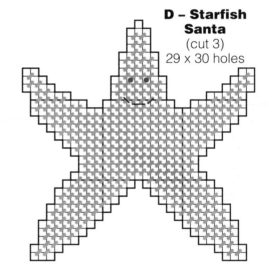

D – Starfish Santa
(cut 3)
29 x 30 holes

F – Beach Ball
(cut 3) 13 x 13 holes

COLOR KEY: Tropical Holiday Decor

Embroidery floss			AMOUNT
■ Dk. Pink			½ yd.
■ Blue			½ yd.

Metallic cord			AMOUNT
▨ Pearl/White			2 yds.

Worsted-weight	Nylon Plus™	Need-loft®	YARN AMOUNT
■ Red	#19	#02	28 yds.
▨ Sand	#47	#16	22 yds.
■ White	#01	#41	18 yds.
▨ Royal	#09	#32	17 yds.
□ Cinnamon	#44	#14	8 yds.
▨ Dk. Green	#31	#27	6 yds.

STITCH KEY:
— Backstitch/Straight Stitch
● French Knot

J – Basket Trim
(cut 1) 4 x 34 holes

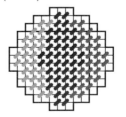

Tropical Holiday Decor

Instructions & photo on pages 146 & 147

COLOR KEY: Tropical Holiday Decor

Embroidery floss			AMOUNT
■ Dk. Pink			1/2 yd.
■ Blue			1/2 yd.

Metallic cord			AMOUNT
■ Pearl/White			2 yds.

Worsted-weight	Nylon Plus™	Need-loft®	YARN AMOUNT
■ Red	#19	#02	28 yds.
■ Sand	#47	#16	22 yds.
■ White	#01	#41	18 yds.
■ Royal	#09	#32	17 yds.
□ Cinnamon	#44	#14	8 yds.
■ Dk. Green	#31	#27	6 yds.

Basket Assembly Diagram

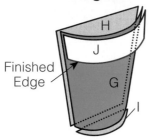

Finished Edge

I – Basket Bottom
(cut 1) 7 x 15 holes

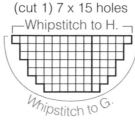

Whipstitch to H.

Whipstitch to G.

A – Wreath Motif (cut 1) 80 x 80 holes

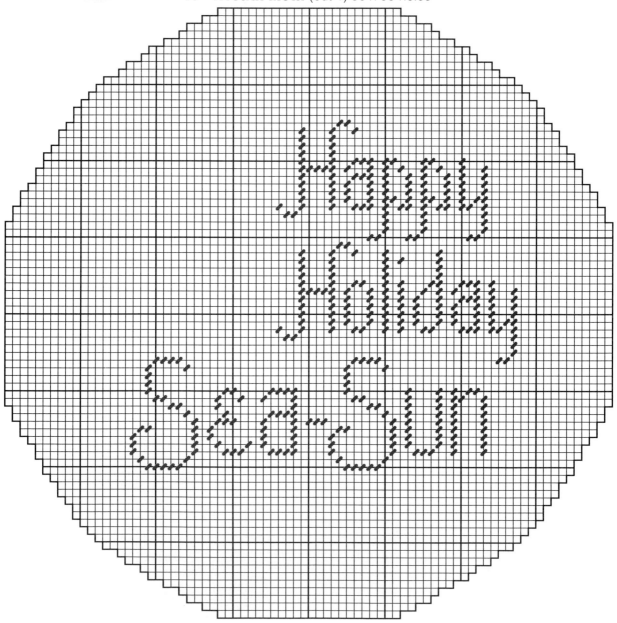

G – Basket Front (cut 1) 25 x 32 holes

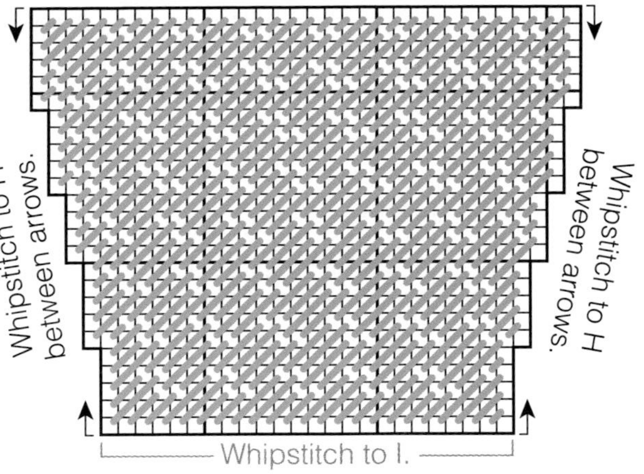
Whipstitch to H between arrows.
Whipstitch to H between arrows.
Whipstitch to I.

H – Basket Back (cut 1) 25 x 25 holes

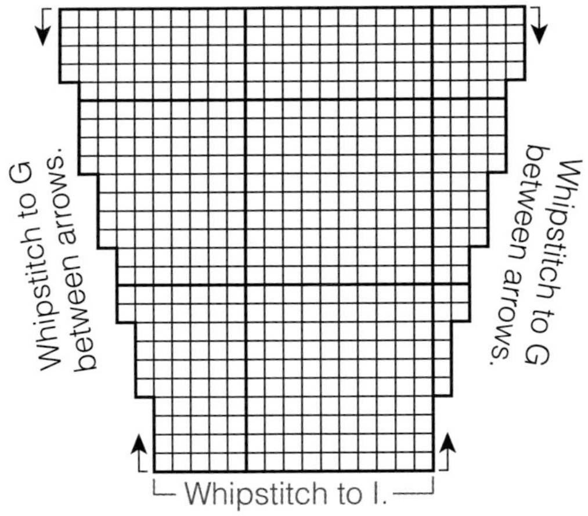
Whipstitch to G between arrows.
Whipstitch to G between arrows.
Whipstitch to I.

Christmas Candles

Continued from page 141

CUTTING INSTRUCTIONS:

A: For top, cut one according to graph.
B: For sides, cut four 30 x 36 holes.

STITCHING INSTRUCTIONS:

1: Using colors indicated and Continental Stitch, work pieces according to graphs. Fill in uncoded areas using black and Continental Stitch. With black, Overcast cutout edges of top.

2: For holly berries, with pearl cotton or six strands floss, sew buttons to pieces as indicated on graphs.

3: With black, Whipstitch pieces together; Overcast unfinished bottom edges.❄

– Designed by Michele Wilcox

COLOR KEY: Christmas Candles

Worsted-weight	Nylon Plus™	Need-loft®	YARN AMOUNT
Black	#02	#00	55 yds.
Pewter	–	#66	16 yds.
Eggshell	#24	#39	12 yds.
Dk. Green	#31	#27	7 yds.
Dusty Rose	#52	#06	6 yds.
Crimson	#53	#42	4 yds.
Tangerine	#15	#11	3 yds.
Dk. Orange	#18	#52	2 yds.

STITCH KEY:

O Button Attachment

A – Top (cut 1) 30 x 30 holes

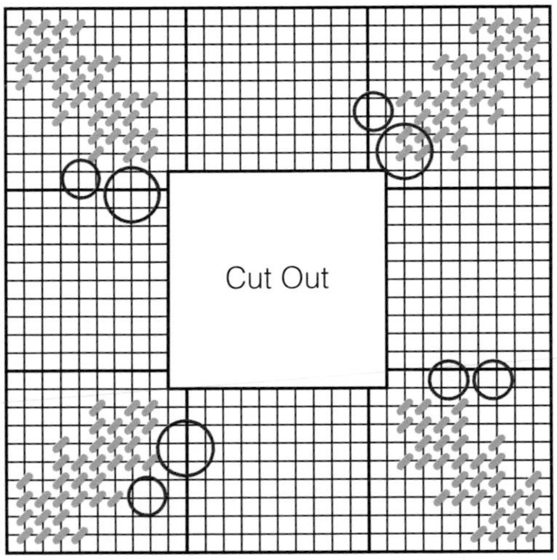
Cut Out

B – Side (cut 4) 30 x 36 holes

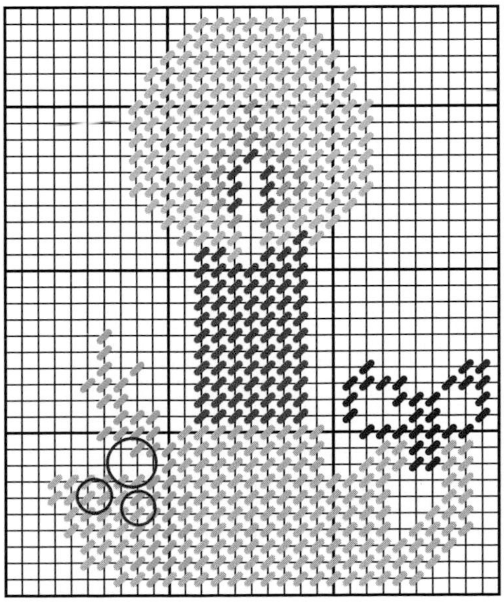

General Instructions

BASIC INSTRUCTIONS TO GET YOU STARTED

Most plastic canvas stitchers love getting their projects organized before they even step out the door in search of supplies. A few moments of careful planning can make the creation of your project even more fun.

First of all, prepare your work area. You will need a flat surface for cutting and assembly, and you will need a place to store your materials. Good lighting is essential, and a comfortable chair will make your stitching time even more enjoyable.

Do you plan to make one project, or will you be making several of the same item? A materials list appears at the beginning of each pattern. If you plan to make several of the same item, multiply your materials accordingly. Your shopping list is ready.

CANVAS

Most projects can be made using standard-size sheets of canvas. Standard-size sheets of 7-count (7 holes per inch) are always 70 x 90 holes and are about 10½" x 13½". For larger projects, 7-count canvas also comes in 12" x 18" (80 x 120 holes) and 13½" x 22½" (90 x 150 holes) sheets. Other shapes are available in 7-count, including circles, diamonds, purse forms and ovals.

10-count canvas (10 holes per inch) comes only in standard-size sheets, which vary slightly depending on brand. They are 10½" x 13½" (106 x 136 holes) or 11" x 14" (108 x 138 holes).

5-count canvas (5 holes per inch) and 14-count (14 holes per inch) sheets are also available.

Some canvas is soft and pliable, while other canvas is stiffer and more rigid. To prevent canvas from cracking during or after stitching, you'll want to choose pliable canvas for projects that require shaping, like round baskets with curved handles. For easier shaping, warm canvas pieces with a blow-dry hair dryer to soften; dip in cool water to set. If your project is a box or an item that will stand alone, stiffer canvas is more suitable.

Both 7- and 10-count canvas sheets are available in a rainbow of colors. Most designs can be stitched on colored as well as clear canvas. When a pattern does not specify color in the materials list, you can assume clear canvas was used in the photographed model. If you'd like to stitch only a portion of the design, leaving a portion unstitched, use colored canvas to coordinate with yarn colors.

Buy the same brand of canvas for each entire project. Different brands of canvas may differ slightly in the distance between each bar.

MARKING & COUNTING TOOLS

To avoid wasting canvas, careful cutting of each piece is important. For some pieces with square corners, you might be comfortable cutting the canvas without marking it beforehand. But for pieces with lots of angles and cutouts, you may want to mark your canvas before cutting.

Always count before you mark and cut. To count holes on the graphs, look for the bolder lines showing each ten holes. These ten-count lines begin in the lower left-hand corner of each graph and are on the graph to make counting easier. To count holes on the canvas, you may use your tapestry needle, a toothpick or a plastic hair roller pick. Insert the needle or pick slightly in each hole as you count.

Most stitchers have tried a variety of marking tools and have settled on a favorite, which may be crayon, permanent marker, grease pencil or ball point pen. One of the best marking tools is a fine-point overhead projection marker, available at office supply stores. The ink is dark and easy to see and washes off completely with water. After cutting and before stitching, it's important to remove all marks so they won't stain yarn as you stitch or show through stitches later. Cloth and paper toweling removes grease pencil and crayon marks, as do fabric softener sheets that have already been used in your dryer.

SUPPLIES

Yarn, canvas, needles, cutters and most other supplies needed to complete the projects in this book are available at craft and needlework stores and through mail order catalogs. Other supplies are available at fabric, hardware and discount stores. For mail order information, see page 159.

CUTTING TOOLS

You may find it very helpful to have several tools on hand for cutting canvas. When cutting long, straight sections, scissors, craft cutters or kitchen shears are the fastest and easiest to use. For cutting out detailed areas and trimming nubs, you may like using manicure scissors or nail clippers. Many stitchers love using Ultimate Plastic Canvas Cutters, available only from *The Needlecraft Shop* catalog. If you prefer laying your canvas flat when cutting, try a craft knife and cutting surface – self-healing mats designed for sewing and kitchen cutting boards work well.

YARN AND OTHER STITCHING MATERIALS

You may choose two-ply nylon plastic canvas yarn (the color numbers of two popular brands are found in the general materials lists and Color Keys) or four-ply worsted-weight yarn for stitching on 7-count canvas. There are about 42 yards per ounce of plastic canvas yarn and 50 yards per ounce of worsted-weight yarn.

Worsted-weight yarn is widely available and comes in wool, acrylic, cotton and blends. If you decide to use worsted-weight yarn, choose 100% acrylic for best coverage. Select worsted-weight yarn by color instead of the color names or numbers found in the Color Keys. Projects stitched with worsted-weight yarn often "fuzz" after use. "Fuzz" can be removed by shaving it off with a fabric shaver to make your project look new again.

Plastic canvas yarn comes in about 60 colors and is a favorite of many plastic canvas designers. These yarns "wear" well both while stitching and in the finished product. When buying plastic canvas yarn, shop using the color names or numbers found in the Color Keys, or select colors of your choice.

To cover 5-count canvas, use a doubled strand of worsted-weight or plastic canvas yarn.

Choose sport-weight yarn or #3 pearl cotton for stitching on 10-count canvas. To cover 10-count canvas using six-strand embroidery floss, use 12 strands held together. Single and double plies of yarn will also cover 10-count and can be used for embroidery or accent stitching worked over needlepoint stitches – simply separate worsted-weight yarn into 2-ply or plastic canvas yarn into 1-ply. Nylon plastic canvas yarn does not perform as well as knitting worsted when separated and can be frustrating to use, but it is possible. Just use short lengths, separate into single plies and twist each ply slightly.

Embroidery floss or #5 pearl cotton can also be used for embroidery, and each covers 14-count canvas well.

Metallic cord is a tightly-woven cord that comes in dozens of glittering colors. Some are solid-color metallics, including gold and silver, and some have colors interwoven with gold or silver threads. If your metallic cord has a white core, the core may be removed for super-easy stitching. To do so, cut a length of cord; grasp center core fibers with tweezers or fingertips and pull. Core slips out easily. Though the sparkly look of metallics will add much to your project, you may substitute contrasting colors of yarn.

Natural and synthetic raffia straw will cover 7-count canvas if flattened before stitching. Use short lengths to prevent splitting, and glue ends to prevent unraveling.

CUTTING CANVAS

Follow all Cutting Instructions, Notes and labels above graphs to cut canvas. Each piece is labeled with a letter of the alphabet. Square-sided pieces are cut according to hole count, and some may not have a graph.

Unlike sewing patterns, graphs are not designed to be used as actual patterns but rather as counting, cutting and stitching guides. Therefore, graphs may not be actual size. Count the holes on the graph (see Marking & Counting Tools on page 154), mark your canvas to match, then cut. The old carpenters' adage – "Measure twice, cut once" – is good advice. Trim off the nubs close to the bar, and trim all corners diagonally.

For large projects, as you cut each piece, it is a good idea to label it with its letter and name. Use sticky labels, or fasten scrap paper notes through the canvas with a twist tie or a quick stitch with a scrap of yarn. To stay organized, you many want to store corresponding pieces together in zip-close bags.

If you want to make several of a favorite design to give as gifts or sell at bazaars, make cutting canvas easier and faster by making a master pattern. From colored canvas, cut out one of each piece required. For duplicates, place the colored canvas on top of clear canvas and cut out. If needed, secure the canvas pieces together with paper fasteners, twist ties or yarn. By using this method, you only have to count from the graphs once.

If you accidentally cut or tear a bar or two on your canvas, don't worry! Boo-boos can usually be repaired in one of several ways: heat the tip of a metal skewer and melt the canvas back together; glue torn bars with a tiny drop of craft glue, super glue or hot glue; or reinforce the torn section with a separate piece of canvas placed at the back of your work. When reinforcing with extra canvas, stitch through both thicknesses.

NEEDLES & OTHER STITCHING TOOLS

Blunt-end tapestry needles are used for stitching plastic canvas. Choose a No. 16 needle for stitching 5- and 7-count, a No. 18 for stitching 10-count and a No. 24 for stitching 14-count canvas. A small pair of embroidery scissors for snipping yarn is handy. Try using needle-nosed jewelry pliers for pulling the needle through several thicknesses of canvas and out of tight spots too small for your hand.

STITCHING THE CANVAS

Stitching Instructions for each section are found after the Cutting Instructions. First, refer to the illustrations of basic stitches found on page 157 to familiarize yourself with the stitches used. Illustrations will be found near the graphs for pieces worked using special stitches. Follow the numbers on the tiny graph beside the illustration to make each stitch – bring your needle up from the back of the work on odd numbers and down through the front of the work on the even numbers.

Before beginning, read the Stitching Instructions to get an overview of what you'll be doing. You'll find that some pieces are stitched using colors and stitches indicated on graphs, and for other pieces you will be given a color and stitch to use to cover the entire piece.

Cut yarn lengths between 18" and 36". Thread needle; do not tie a knot in the end. Bring your needle up through the canvas from the back, leaving a short length of yarn on the wrong side of the canvas. As you begin to stitch, work over this short length of yarn. If you are beginning with Continental Stitches, leave a 1" length, but if you are working longer stitches, leave a longer length.

In order for graph colors to contrast well, graph colors may not match yarn colors. For instance, a light yellow may be selected to represent the metallic cord color gold, or a light blue may represent white yarn.

When following a graph showing several colors, you may want to work all the stitches of one color at the same time. Some stitchers prefer to work with several colors at once by threading each on a separate needle and letting the yarn not being used hang on the wrong side of the work. Either way, remember that strands of yarn run across the wrong side of the work may show through the stitches from the front.

As you stitch, try to maintain an even tension on the yarn. Loose stitches will look uneven, and tight stitches will let the canvas show through. If your yarn twists as you work, you may want to let your needle and yarn hang and untwist occasionally.

When you end a section of stitching or finish a thread, weave the yarn through the back side of your last few stitches, then trim it off.

CONSTRUCTION & ASSEMBLY

After all pieces of an item needing assembly are stitched, you will find the order of assembly is listed in the Stitching Instructions and sometimes illustrated in Diagrams found with the graphs. For best results, join pieces in the order written. Refer to the Stitch Key and to the directives near the graphs for precise attachments.

FINISHING TIPS

To combat glue strings when using a hot glue gun, practice a swirling motion as you work. After placing the drop of glue on your work, lift the gun slightly and swirl to break the stream of glue, as if you were making an ice cream cone. Have a cup of water handy when gluing. For those times that you'll need to touch the glue, first dip your finger into the water just enough to dampen it. This will minimize the glue sticking to your finger, and it will cool and set the glue more quickly.

To attach beads, use a bit more glue to form a cup around the bead. If too much shows after drying, use a craft knife to trim off excess glue.

Scotchguard® or other fabric protectors may be used on your finished projects. However, avoid using a permanent marker if you plan to use a fabric protector, and be sure to remove all other markings before stitching. Fabric protectors can cause markings to bleed, staining yarn.

FOR MORE INFORMATION

Sometimes even the most experienced needlecrafters can find themselves having trouble following instructions. If you have difficulty completing your project, write to Plastic Canvas Editors, *The Needlecraft Shop*, 23 Old Pecan Road, Big Sandy, Texas 75755.

Stitch Guide

NEEDLEPOINT STITCHES

CONTINENTAL STITCH
can be used to stitch designs or fill in background areas.

RYA KNOT
is used to fill in background areas or as an embroidery stitch to add a loopy or fringed texture. Stitch over two bars leaving a loop, then stitch over adjacent bars to anchor the loop.

LONG STITCH
is a horizontal or vertical stitch used to stitch designs or fill in background areas. Can be stitched over two or more bars.

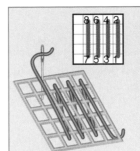

OVERCAST
is used to finish edges. Stitch two or three times in corners for complete coverage.

REVERSE CONTINENTAL STITCH
can be used to stitch designs or fill in background areas.

WHIPSTITCH
is used to join two or more pieces together.

SCOTCH STITCH

BEAD ATTACHMENT

SLANTED GOBELIN STITCH
can be used to stitch designs or fill in background areas. Can be stitched over two or more bars in vertical or horizontal rows.

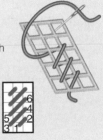

EMBROIDERY STITCHES

BACKSTITCH
is usually used as an embroidery stitch to outline or add detail. Stitches can be any length and go in any direction.

STRAIGHT STITCH
is usually used as an embroidery stitch to add detail. Stitches can be any length and can go in any direction. Looks like Backstitch except stitches do not touch.

CROSS STITCH
can be used as a needlepoint stitch or as an embroidery stitch stitched over background stitches with contrasting yarn or floss.

LARK'S HEAD KNOT

FRENCH KNOT
is usually used as an embroidery stitch to add detail. Can be made in one hole or over a bar. If dot on graph is in hole as shown, come up and go down with needle in same hole.

Acknowledgments

We would like to express our appreciation to the many people who helped create this book. Our special thanks go to each of the talented designers who contributed original designs and to our extraordinary models, Trevor and Micah Godfrey (back cover) and Donna Robertson, our two wonderful Santas: Bill Bessonett (cover) and Clayton Taylor who patiently posed for each photograph. The beautiful photography locations in Texas were provided by Bill and Jo Bessonett, Tyler; Craig and Jan Jaynes, Kilgore; Ed and Elaine Snavely, Tyler and Bill and Ruth Whitaker, Tyler. A special thanks to Vic Green, Festive Fotos in Mesquite, for sharing Santa's wonderful wardrobe and Dale Miller, Broadway Florist in Big Sandy, for photo props.

We also wish to express our gratitude to the following manufacturers for their generous contribution of materials and supplies for some of the featured projects:

CHARMING ST. NICK

Christmas Spirits: Darice® canvas; The Beadery® cabochons; Creative Crystal Company charms, beads and rhinestones; Kreinik metallic braid; Madeira Glissen Gloss™ Estaz; DMC® pearl cotton; Spinrite® yarn.

Country Santa: Darice® canvas; Westrim® Crafts jingle bells; Kunin Felt Rainbow™ hair; Aleene's™ Designer Tacky Glue; Rhode Island Textiles RibbonFloss™; One & Only Creations® Bumples™ yarn hair; Bernat® Plastic Canvas Cotton Yarn.

Santa's Watching: Darice® canvas; Uniek® Crafts Needloft® yarn.

Nesting Santas: DMC® pearl cotton; Uniek® Crafts Needloft® yarn.

Santa's Place Mat: Uniek® Crafts Needloft® yarn.

Tyrolean Match Holder: DMC® pearl cotton; Spinrite® yarn.

FROSTY FRIENDS

I Love Snow: Rhode Island Textiles metallic ribbon; Spinrite® yarn.

Mini Frosty Basket: DMC® pearl cotton; Uniek® Crafts Needloft® yarn.

Penguin Party: Uniek® Crafts Needloft® yarn.

Christmas Wall Hanging: Darice® canvas; DMC® pearl cotton; Uniek® Crafts Needloft® yarn.

YULETIDE TRADITIONS

Bells & Bows: Darice® canvas and metallic cord; Uniek® Crafts Needloft® yarn.

Poinsettias 'round the Room: Darice® canvas, metallic cord and Nylon Plus™ yarn.

Season's Greetings Cap: Uniek® Crafts metallic cord and Needloft® yarn.

Ornament Coasters: Darice® canvas; Kreinik metallic braid; J & P Coats® plastic canvas yarn.

Gift Wrapped Doorstop: Darice® canvas and Nylon Plus™ yarn.

Country Christmas Kitchen: Uniek® Crafts Needloft® yarn.

GIFTS FROM SANTA

Merry Lights Earrings: DMC® pearl cotton.

Candy Cane Earrings: Darice® canvas; Rhode Island Textiles Ribbon Floss™; Kreinik blending filament; DMC® embroidery floss.

"Ho Ho Ho" Pin: Darice® canvas and raffia straw; Kreinik metallic ribbon; Uniek® Crafts Needloft® yarn.

Nutcracker Soldier: Uniek® Crafts Needloft® yarn.

Chef Piggy: Darice® canvas and metallic cord; The Beadery® cabochons; DMC® pearl cotton; Uniek® Crafts Needloft® yarn.

Rustic Lodge Canisters: Darice® canvas.

CHRISTMAS SPIRIT

Celestial Messengers: Darice® canvas and doll heads; Wrights® ribbon; Zucker Feathers; Fibre-Craft® terry stems; Mill Hill seed beads from Gay Bowles Sales, Inc.; One & Only Creations® Mini-Curl™ doll hair; Aleene's™ Thick Designer Tacky Glue; Kreinik metallic braid; Anchor® pearl cotton.

Angelic Doorstop: Darice® canvas and metallic cord; DMC® pearl cotton; Uniek® Crafts Needloft® yarn.

Musical Spirits: Offray ribbon; Kreinik metallic braid; Uniek® Crafts Needloft® yarn.

Stained Glass Tote: Darice® canvas and metallic cord; Uniek® Crafts Needloft® yarn.

Bejeweled Angel: Darice® canvas and metallic cord; The Beadery® gemstones; Wrights® trims; FibreCraft® doll parts; Uniek® Crafts Needloft® yarn.

Christmas Advent Calendar: DMC® pearl cotton; Uniek® Crafts Needloft® yarn.

SANTA TREATS

Doorknob Basket: Darice® canvas and raffia straw.

Christmas Tic-Tac-Toe: Uniek® Crafts Needloft® yarn.

Bathtime Fun: Darice® canvas; Uniek® Crafts Needloft® yarn.

Clown Collector: Darice® canvas; One & Only Creations® Maxi-Curl™ doll hair; DMC® pearl cotton, Spinrite® yarn.

FESTIVE TRIMMINGS

Lil' Package Ornaments: Rainbow Gallery metallic ribbon; Uniek® Crafts Needloft® yarn.

Yuletide Warmers: Darice® canvas and Nylon Plus™ yarn.

Snowy Evergreen: Darice® canvas and Fashion Lites battery-operated musical twinkle lights.

Christmas Candles: Darice® canvas; DMC® pearl cotton; Uniek® Crafts Needloft® yarn.

Shimmering Shapes: Uniek® Crafts canvas and metallic cord.

Tropical Holiday Decor: Darice® canvas and Pearlized Metallic Cord; Anchor® embroidery floss; Uniek® Crafts Needloft® yarn.

Pearls & Lace: Darice® canvas; Offray ribbon; Kreinik blending filament.

Pattern Index

Angelic Doorstop, 98

Bathtime Fun, 117
Bejeweled Angel, 106
Bells & Bows, 52
Bougainvillea Frame, 78

Chef Piggy, 82
Candy Cane Earrings, 72
Celestial Messengers, 96
Christmas Advent Calendar, 108
Christmas Candles, 141
Christmas Candy Boxes, 122
Christmas Spirits, 8
Christmas Tic-Tac-Toe, 116
Christmas Wall Hanging, 44
Clown Collector, 120
Country Christmas Kitchen, 64
Country Decor, 68
Country Santa, 12

Doorknob Basket, 114

Elegant Snow Angels, 134

Festive Touches, 140

Gift Wrapped Doorstop, 63

"Ho Ho Ho" Pin, 73

I Love Snow, 38

Lil' Package Ornaments, 136

Merry Lights Earrings, 72
Mini Frosty Basket, 39
Musical Spirits, 100

Nesting Santas, 20
Nutcracker Soldier, 80

Ornament Coasters, 62

Pearls & Lace, 148
Penguin Party, 40
Percival Penguin, 32

Poinsettias 'round the Room, 54
Precious Pet, 74
Pretty Pinecones, 132

Rustic Lodge Canisters, 89

Santa's Place Mat, 22
Santa's Watching, 14
Season's Greetings Cap, 56
Shimmering Shapes, 144
Snowy Evergreen, 138
Southern Belle, 124
Stained Glass Tote, 103

Tropical Holiday Decor, 147
Tyrolean Match Holder, 26

Warm Winter Friends, 46
Winter Wizard, 24
Wintery Wreath, 34

Yuletide Warmers, 137

Designer Index

Blizzard, Vicki, 8, 82, 120
Burch, Trina Taylor, 56, 100

Celia Lange Designs, 26, 38
Chamberlain, Glenda, 147

Davis, Dianne, 96
DiGeorge, Anne, 68

Fanton, Darla J., 12
Fox, Jacquelyn, 14

Hall, Patricia, 78

Keel, Debby, 103
Keklock, Joyce, 122
Kennebeck, Kathleen, 72, 73

Lampin, Jimmy & Jessie, 107
Leck, Cherie Marie, 20, 40, 64, 72, 108, 116, 136, 144

Marshall, Nancy, 89, 114, 137
Miller Maxfield, Sandra, 80, 107

Nelson, Judy L., 124

Petrina, Robin, 34

Radla, Betty, 52, 117
Ray, Diane T., 54, 74, 138

Suber, Kimberly A., 140

Walter, Rosemarie, 62, 148
Wilcox, Michele, 22, 39, 45, 63, 98, 141
Will, Robin, 24, 32, 46, 132, 134